Introduction

Ikigai: The Japanese Art of Living

Just as the whole world is influenced by the personality of a single person, in the same way, there are very few countries which have influenced other countries of the world. There are very few countries which are known for their lifestyle. Today, I wish to tell you about a country about which, it is said that its people live the longest lives. That country is Japan.

Not only do the Japanese live longer lives, but they also remain active longer, live a social life and contribute to the development of their nation. Today, people want to know, how this was possible, and want to learn about the way the Japanese live. This despite the fact that Japan was badly hit during the second world war. Millions of people lost their lives. Many countries had enforced bans. So much so, people in Japan had begun starving to death. Even then, Japan rose to become one of the biggest political and economic power in Asia. How was this possible? This was made possible by the Japanese lifestyle.

Now, you may think what the Japanese lifestyle is. I will explain in detail in the coming chapters, but the name of this art of Japanese living is Ikigai. The people of Japan follow this way of living to make their lives happy and lengthy. The meaning of Ikigai is, "What is the meaning of Life?" The principles of Ikigai help people to find the aim of their life. When you find your Ikigai, that is, the meaning or aim of your life, then you can lead a great life. This book will not only provide you with theoretical ideas, but also how to lead the Ikigai life with practical examples. It is then that you will know what this Japanese way of living actually is. How the people of that country achieve their goals. How they scale great heights in society and achieve a high social standing. What do they eat that they are able to live a long and fruitful life. This book will help you live a successful life and achieve new heights of success every day, and you will enjoy it.

What is Ikigai? Ikigai is the art of living life in a way that a person is always inspired to remain focused on their goal. The meaning of Ikigai is to make your life meaningful. The people who use the principles of Ikigai always wake up in the morning with a sense of meaning. This is the reason why, despite having been destroyed in the second world war, Japan did not only develop, but also became a nation of longevity. How was all this possible? This was only possible by adopting the principles of Ikigai. If you would like to live a good and meaningful long life, then this book will definitely help you.

–Author

Contents

1. The Art of Staying Young 7

2. The Secret of Not Increasing your Age...............................17

3. Ikigai through Logotherapy 34

4. The Search for Flow..44

5. Longevity Masters 56

6. Ikigai Food Culture...73

7. Rhythmic Exercises 84

8. Worry and Tension 100

Chapter 1

The Art of Staying Young

Japanese life is very interesting and creative too. If you once understand the rule of Ikigai that the Japanese have adopted in their lives, then you can also live a long and valuable life. You may remember that 24% of the Japanese population stay alive till 100 years. What do they do to stay young? First of all, let me tell you that due to the adoption of the rules of Ikigai, they recognise the motive of their lives. That is why, they follow concepts of Ikigai in their diets, daily living, work and culture. Let us find out what exactly Japanese people do to stay young.

Motive of Life

In this world many people are living their life based on their individual thinking. Everyone is in a race, competing with others in their life.

Their only aim in life is to try to pull down everyone else. Today, no one has time for anything. Not even for their own family. Everyone is living their lives, but there is no peace or happiness in their lives. You can ask any person: What's the goal of your life? Why are you living? Most of the time you would get an answer like: What do you mean by goal? My aim in life is only to earn money, to be able to feed myself and my family. To enjoy my life before I die. If this question is asked to all people around the world, you will get the same answer from almost 90% people. So, my question to you is, should this and only this, be the meaning of our life? Should we spend our entire, very precious life in just earning money only?

In contrast to most people, Japanese people have the goal for their life planned. To achieve that goal, they change their lifestyle and habits regularly according to their goals. Most people set their goals accordingly their lifestyle. This is the biggest mistake that people make.

Japanese people don't wake up because it is morning, rather, they wake up so that they can go ahead and achieve their goals.

Retirement has No Age

Old age comes to mind, whenever we think of retirement. After retirement most people spend their time at home and get bored, living their monotonous daily routine. Most of the people feel that after retirement life would be dull, boring, and it would be difficult to pass the time. If this is your way of thinking too, change it now. Because Japanese people don't let themselves get retired. When they reach a certain age, they simply set fresh goals for themselves. If you adopt this thought, you too will be looking and feeling young. If you are getting old, simply set some new goals in life.

1. **Setting goals gives satisfaction:** Japanese people always work with their goals in mind. This makes their

life and their country better. Because of this, they stay happy themselves and make others happier too. This is the reason, why the Japanese people stay young and have satisfaction and happiness. The real learning from this is that human life should have some goals definitely.

2. **Real meaning of life:** What is the meaning of life? How do we search for goals, completeness, and a sense of satisfaction in life? Can we achieve the ultimate importance of anything? Most of the people haven't stopped to ponder over these important questions. When they look back and wonder why their contacts have broken, why they feel an emptiness, even though they achieved all, for which they started out. Japanese people are always working towards making life worthwhile. That's why they always look young.

3. **Signs of being actively young:** Many people feel like old persons even though they are young. But Japanese people look younger even when they are old, as they live an active and busy life inspired by their goals. This is the important reason that makes Japan different.

4. **Do your favourite work:** Everyone has some hobbies which they like. Hobbies give us enjoyment. We don't feel bored when we pursue our hobbies. In this vast world, everyone has their own nature and likings. Their hobbies and interests are different. Because of this context, while some people like sweet things, other prefer to eat sour things. Since, there is no word for retirement in the dictionary of the Japanese, they choose to keep on doing their favourite work and their happy lifestyle helps them to live longer.

Food Habits, Ways of Living and Culture

The Japanese are known all over the world to be the most healthy and fit people, and they remain in the limelight because of their lifestyle. Everyone wants to know the secret of their fitness. We know that Japanese people take special care of their diet, and do their physical exercises regularly. Because of their good and healthy diet, they look fit and fine for a longer time. They keep themselves young by adopting the rules of Ikigai.

1. **The Japanese Diet:** Normally Japanese people eat three times a day. But their eating time is very less, as they give more time to their work. Mostly, Japanese eat very little for their breakfast as they have to go for work. Generally, lunch starts at 12 and goes on for one hour. Dinner time is also for one hour. Mostly, the Japanese are known for eating fast. They use Chinese forks for eating. Generally Japanese food is very light.

2. **Tradition of drinking tea:** Tea is one of the favourite drinks of Japan. In Japan, different types of tea are taken from morning to evening, and on every festival. Japan

produces more than 100 types of tea. Maximum people drink green tea. Japanese tea is much healthier and better than our Indian tea, because these people don't add sugar and milk to their tea. When people suffer from different diseases also, they use different types of tea as a cure. The method of making and drinking of each tea is different. There are more than 28 types of green tea which is being drunk in Japan. Different types of tea help in keeping bone, hair and skin, etc. safe for a long time. Besides, tea is rich in antioxidants, so, it keeps the body active, which makes the Japanese, to continue to do work even when they get exhausted.

3. **Walking:** The Japanese like to walk for their most of the works. This is a very special and important part of their lifestyle. Although, there is no scarcity of anything in Japan due to technology development, but still people prefer to travel in public transport rather than by their private vehicles. Because, they believe that by doing so, they keep themselves fit and healthy, as they have to walk much longer for traveling by train or bus. Sometimes, they have to stand while traveling. This makes digestion faster and easy, and the body weight also doesn't increase.

4. **Cleanliness:** In Japan, people pay a lot of attention to cleanliness. That's why Japan is among one of the cleanest countries. When they visit other countries, they take care of cleanliness there also. They believe that cleanliness protects everyone from the diseases and helps maintain mental balance. So, one can be protected from minor diseases very easily by simply following hygiene.

5. **Cheerful way of living:** Sometimes in our life, things don't happen as we wish or think. Some of our dreams and wishes remain unfulfilled. Here, we have to understand

that in the world everything cannot happen according to our wishes. There are certain things which are beyond human control. And, there is no point in worrying or crying over such uncontrollable things. Instead of making life like hell, it is better to live life cheerfully. Japanese people stay young because they don't live a tension filled life.

6. **Light exercises:** Japanese people have found in their studies that light and easy exercises keep natural killer cells more active while hard and strenuous exercises done for a long time decreases their capacity. These changes apply in the same way on hormones responsible for tension and antibodies cells as well. This is why the Japanese eat light food and do light exercises.

7. **Working on the land:** The Japanese like to work on their farmland. This is the reason that they remain energetic and healthy.

8. **Less alcohol:** If you are taking one full glass of alcohol then your body gets 178 calories. This is equal to eating two chocolate biscuits. To burn these calories, you will have to walk briskly for half an hour. When you are regularly drinking alcohol or eating too much, your weight increases rapidly. Food has some nutrients, but there are no nutrients in alcohol. The Japanese drink very less alcohol, so they don't have any obesity problems.

9. **Be young by eating less:** The rule of Japanese life is to eat lesser food, just to fill their half stomach only. Eating more food needs more energy to burn the calories which we have consumed, which decreases our age. To eat less food, it is served in smaller plates. Without any need, one should not eat food, snacks or any other edibles. All Japanese people consume lots of green vegetables.

To Live in Limited Sources

The key to a successful life is: To be successful in any work, the person should have a healthy body. This is because success cannot be gained without being healthy. When a person is healthy, his mind, his power to think, and dedication towards his work is always in excellent form. Only then can he would be successful. The Japanese know that in their country, there are limited life resources, so they have learned to live while making use of very little amounts of things. This helps them keep their age always young.

1. **To help each other:** To help others is a very good quality to have. We cannot stress enough the positive aspects of kindness. We should all try to become such a person whom people will remember in the time of need. The Japanese people believe that to help each other is also a form of Ikigai. Helping each other has become a part of their culture. Because of this feeling also, people live longer.

2. **Time Management:** How you spend your time decides the quality of your life. Time management and pre planning helps a person to be tension free. We should adopt the style of working that brings the direct changes in how we use our time. The main rule of time management is to put your time in the important work or those works which are helpful to get your goal. The Japanese do their time management very well, so their life is happy and they remain young.

Attachment with Life

There is no set definition for relations. Even if we try, we can't give any definition which can define the relationships deeply. It doesn't mean that relations are tangled. The definition

of relations is one which can't be understood, but the reality is that relationships are the big scale of life's success, which can't be expressed in words. Some relations are such that can bring changes in your life. But, there are some relations which we may repent to be attached with. The pinch of any such relations remains lifelong. The secret of happy life of Japanese is the attachment with life.

1. **Friendly Behaviour:** If you want to live longer then say goodbye to any kind of animosity. According to Ikigai, one should be friendly with everyone in one's lifetime. That's why they stay friendly with each other, and this also helps the Japanese people to live longer.

2. **Assemble for one motive:** Cooperation is a person's birth need. A person's existence, development and life are all dependent on cooperation. Hunger is the basic need of a person. For their satisfaction, they need to contact different people, and this is a fact that everyone knows. Similarly, they need many other things, for which it is important to get others' cooperation. The Japanese believe in a cooperative life system and living together.

3. **Social service:** Cooperation is a person's birth need. A person's existence, development and life are all dependent on cooperation. Hunger is the basic need of a person. For their satisfaction, they need to contact different people, and this is a fact that everyone knows. Similarly, they need many other things, for which it is important to get others' cooperation. The Japanese lifestyle is closely associated with social service. This keeps them happy and living longer.

4. **To work together in adverse conditions:** Of course, life doesn't stop anywhere and time is always changing. So, we should maintain our mental balance. We should use our brains and face life's adverse times with patience. The Japanese believe in facing the adverse conditions of life in a united manner, together. This is their unique and important style adapted from the concept of Ikigai.

5. **To help each other:** The aim of Japanese people's life is to help others physically, mentally and in every manner possible. It is always seen that those people who help others, have less tension in their mind. They feel mental peace and joy. They feel spirituality attached to them, and their life is satisfactory. While those people who are engaged in competition and comparison always feel tensed. The Japanese are always ready to help others on their part. This makes them extremely happy and energetic. It might be the secret of a long life.

6. **Collect monthly community donations:** To help other people is a very good quality. We can't say enough on the positive aspects of kindness. We all try to become such a person whom people remember in their time of need. The Japanese organise community feasts, community games and other community activities by collecting community

donations. It brings a quality of prosperity to their life. One single person cannot help everyone but groups can help numerous people.

7. **Tension free life:** It is not possible to have a tension free life in modern times. Life has its daily problems. Whether one is poor, middle-class, rich, or super rich, everyone is troubled in some way or another. And tensions make their body hollow. The reactions of people to their problems create tension. Tension is now an inseparable part of life. The Japanese remove their tension by sharing within their community. When you don't have any tensions, life expectancy will increase. This is the rule of Ikigai.

◻

Chapter 2

The secret for not aging

If you have some goals in your life then you live longer compared to others who don't. Having a longer life is not a secret. One's lifeline can be extended by having a set of commitments and taking care of some special things. It doesn't matter, at what age one decides the goals of one's life. Physical activities are more important than other activities. But people do just the opposite in their old age, that is, they decrease their physical activities and start sedentary life. This is the reason that, in older age, people become sick. Whatever the age, physical activities are important for a person to be healthy, cheerful and energetic.

Stay Young in Body and Mind

To be ageing is not such a disease which is curable. We have to look and feel good, but it doesn't mean we should be able to turn back the clock. We are the product of our genes. How much care we took in the earlier times, our body becomes accordingly. Accept the positive things of changing your lifestyle. Be happy and look happy. If you complain about something in any certain period or age, now learn to forgive and have a smiling visage. The most important thing is to keep your mind and body young.

Everyone wants to live a good life. This would be possible only if they are physically and mentally healthy. Mental health is as important as physical health. But in the present time, there are many such issues which affect the mental health of people directly.

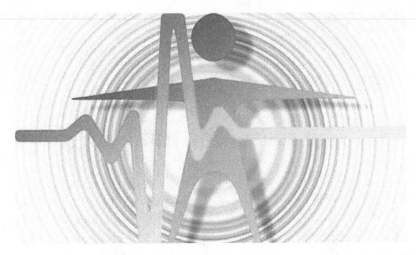

But you can do some exercises for better mental health which will help you to stay mentally healthy. Let me tell you that a person will feel physically healthy only when he would be mentally happy. So, for any person, it is very important to be mentally healthy, on which basis he lives his entire life.

What is Mental Health?

People lose their thinking power when their mental health is not good. They are unable to concentrate on their work. In this situation, first their behaviour changes, which affects their health badly. Their appetite may decrease gradually, and they may get tense. This makes them physically sick. And they could suffer from chronic diseases like high blood pressure or diabetes. So, it is very important to do exercises and yoga for mental health to stay physically healthy.

1. **Mental Exercises:** Every day in the morning when you wake up, your health conditions determine your daily routine. Any bodily disease weakens our enthusiasm, and puts obstructions in the way of our doing our daily chores. There are many yoga exercises which can help

you to stay healthy. Especially you have to note that physical exercise is simply a step towards the larger goal of the complete goal of overall health. Your mental health is equally important. Your mind plays an important part in doing your daily work. Your reaction capacities, understanding capacities, feeling capacities, and working normally all are connected to your brain. Mostly, we can't understand that, like the other body parts, the brain also needs energy and nutrition every day. Just as physical exercises are important to keep your body fit, mental exercises are equally important for mental health.

2. **Community sports:** Sports are an inseparable part of our life. Sports are not only important for physical development and health but they help our mental development also. Sports bring feelings of unity, discipline, and patriotism in us.

3. **Conversation with people:** If you want your mental health to be balanced, don't be quiet about your tensions or problems. Instead, you should get rid of the tensions and problems by talking to the people around you. By doing this, you will feel fresh. If possible, talk to people

close to you about your feelings, fears, and problems, so these should not burden your mental health.

4. **Curiosity:** Curiosity or eagerness is willingness to know, which is seen in expressing, checking, and learning. This is natural in human beings and many other animals. Curiosity is the main reason which leads to scientific inventions and studies. Curiosity is the will to invent such things which are unknown to everyone. Basically, it focuses on the attention of those things which do not trouble people or which don't mean anything for them. The persons with more curiosity live longer.

5. **Mental training:** Largely, mental training and investigation affects people's psychological health in an alert and purposeful manner. Mental training can be done in any situation; like as- Class, the sports field, complexes or public places, you can even do it near a river or a mountain, tourist spots, etc.

6. **Changes in work style:** The secret of a long life is not only in the outer personality but in the person's workstyle, behaviour, and keeping positive thoughts for others. Life can be boring, with the same style, same attitude, same thinking you cannot bring freshness in your life. This type of lifestyle is boring, as there are no new thoughts. There is no enthusiasm. There is no solution. There is no such thing like success. In this matter, to make life interesting, you will have to change your style, your systems and yourself.

7. **Positive views:** Conditions are sometimes favourable and sometimes unfavourable. Life has its own ups and downs. Everyone may be a victim at some point of time. So, don't be sad in these situations. We don't have to run. But, we have to face the challenges life gives us. One

more thing is that we don't have, to be discouraged in facing adverse conditions. The situation is as simple as it is complex. In simple words, it is normal. Sometimes we get discouraged by little things. We get scared. We become weak. But we will have to move ahead with self confidence in all the adverse situations.

8. **Will for learning:** There is no fix age for learning. It is a never ending process. The direct relation of learning is connected to a positive and enthusiastic attitude in life. You should value yourself. Identify minutely your capabilities, nature, behaviour and value them. Search for happiness in little things. Search the moments to thank God, the conditions you live in and the persons around you. Gradually, your attitude would become positive. You will have the inclination towards learning new things. Once you develop this will power to learn inside you, it will become a part of your nature.

Tension reduces Life

Modern human beings have one of the biggest challenges that is their health. Today's lifestyle and habits are reducing the

average age of people. Earlier it was said that humans have 100 years of age but now in most of the countries the average age is reduced to less than 60 years. Though studies claim that if humans can get rid of their tensions, they can live upto 150 years. Tension has a big impact on the lifespan. Not only this, the quality of a person's life also gets affected because of tension.

Hormone levels also keep increasing because of tension. Out of the hormones in the body, adrenaline and cortisol are the main ones. Continuous tensions convert into depression. Depression is a serious situation. Though it is not a disease but it's a sign that your body and life are unbalanced. Depression is supposed to be associated with mental diseases but its symptoms can be seen from outside also.

Signs of Tension

- **Lack of Concentration:** The main sign of depression is that a person always seems worried, and is not able to concentrate in any work. There is no simple sadness but not concentrating on any work, no interest, no feeling of happiness nor even sadness feeling, are signs of depression.

- **Negativity:** Depression affects a person's mind in many ways. Because of this, a person always keeps on thinking negatively. When this reaches to a maximum, a person feels his life is aimless. Besides this, always having a feeling of inferiority is also a sign of depression.

How to remove Tension

Everyone is surrounded by tensions in today's busy world. Today, there is cut throat competition in every field, so from a small child to pensioners, everyone has lots of tension. There can be many causes of this tension-- for children it is study, for adults it's the children's upbringing, household responsibilities, disagreements in family or office, business problems etc. This means no one can say that he is living a tension free life.

Tips to remove Tension

The limit of tension or problems is that we get sick of some diseases. There are some diseases which can be caused because of it:

- Depression
- Heart disease
- High sugar level
- Irritating behaviour, short temper
- Mental diseases, etc

To stay away from these diseases, the question arises in our mind that how do we escape from tension? And how can we be happy? Answers of these questions can be got by adopting these simple methods in our life style:

Make a daily routine: All of us get surrounded by such problems where we have to not only face them but to prove ourselves the best, be it office meeting or examination. So, we should follow one daily routine instead of being tense because of the difficulties of the situation. One correct daily routine is the solution of your daily problems and makes lots of things easier. Then you will be able to face the problems in the same way like your normal day's activities.

Start your day early: Make a habit to get up early in the morning, so that your daily routine will start on time and your attention will be on your work. You will be able to escape from lots of useless tensions like traffic, getting late, etc. There will be no tension for you.

Make a list: Make the list of all the works which make you happy doing them, and you will get positive energy. Along with making a list for daily works and finish them all without forgetting. This techniques will help to lessen and remove your tensions.

Learn to accept the problems: If you are stuck in some bad and hard conditions, then accept them rather than moving away from them. Try to get over the bad time by facing it. In this way, you will have the strength to face the problems and fight the difficulties. Your self-confidence will increase and there will be positivity in you. So, you will be standing stronger in future problems and will have less tensions.

Take care of yourself: If we are in some difficult and tense situations, we stop caring for ourselves, and keep on thinking about that danger all the time. Because of it sometimes we forget to eat properly or eat unhealthy food which is not good for us. We don't sleep well in the night. This does not solve the problems but our health gets affected and deteriorates. So, it is important that we should stay healthy. If we are healthy, we will stay tension free, and then we will be able to solve the problem.

Meditation: Doing meditation is the best way to remove the tension. Daily meditation for 20 or 30 minutes is enough, for a tension free life. It is very helpful to get rid of anger and irritation you feel. This also increases your concentration power.

One work at one time: Do only one work at a time. Do not take the responsibility to finish all the works on yourself, lest not a single work should be completed on time. Or it may even be faulty. Take one work in your hand and finish it on time. This way work will be completed fast, with no mistakes. So, there will be no tension and you will be happy.

Stay away from disruptions and disturbances: At the time when you are working, then don't check your email, mobile, or social media notifications, because by checking these your attention in your work gets disrupted, and it will take more time to finish the work. You won't have much time for other works and you would be in tension, as you haven't completed your work.

Concentration: When you are doing some work, then your aim should be to finish it with full concentration. When you concentrate fully on one work, then only it gets completed fast. Besides, you should not mix many things together, so that you are able to do work with concentration.

Question yourself: If you are feeling tense about some matters, then do self-interview to remove the tension. Ask yourself such questions which you have in mind related to that problem. The answers of these questions will help to get yourself out of this problem, and you will be able to stay away from tension.

Do not postpone the work: Postponing or procrastinating any work is a very bad habit. It's 100% true that tomorrow never comes. Nobody knows how much work you would have for tomorrow. Whether you will get time to do the postponed works or not. If yesterday's work couldn't get done today also, then you would be in tension. So, you should never wait till the actual deadline.

Take a deep breath: While resting, taking deep breaths helps you to fight any mental tension. Whenever you are in tension, then first pause for some time and take a deep long breath. This technique proves helpful for your mind to be tension free.

Do regular exercise: Daily exercise not only keeps you physically healthy but also makes you mentally stronger. It also helps in reducing stress hormones of the body. And then we can live a cheerful and tension free life.

Eat cheerfully: Very often it happens, we don't eat breakfast and lunch in the haste of work. If we eat at all, then also we take this as some task to be completed. So, we don't get sufficient and required nutrition. Therefore, never leave breakfast or lunch, and whenever you eat, have it peacefully and relish it. You will experience peace of mind. It will make you happy and thus you will be tension free.

Complete your hobbies: Whenever you feel boring in doing work and feel exhausted, then spend time in doing works of your interest and hobby. You will be happy to devote time to your hobbies and you will become tension free. After that, you will do your work with double enthusiasm.

Have sufficient sleep: It is important to take sound and sufficient sleep in the night, so as to get up early in the morning with full freshness and energy for daylong work and become winner. Because, if all your tasks be done correctly, then there would be no tension and you will be happy.

Share the problems: It is said that shared happiness increases the joy and shared sorrows decrease the burden. So, if you are troubled by something, share it with your family members and good friends. It is quite possible you would have some solution. If not the complete solution, at least you would feel lighter and have less tension.

Spend time with family: At present, many people stay away from family because of their livelihood, or even when they stay with family, they don't give enough time to their children and other family members. This creates a communication gap between family members and causes tension. So, it's important that you should give time to your life partner and family members.

Have vacations or a picnic with them, tell your childhood stories to your children and have fun with them. Take interest in their studies, hobbies, and know their problems. It will make your relationship stronger and you won't be affected by tensions and would be happy.

Stay with positive people: It is very important to know with whom you spend the time, to find a solution for your tensions. Because if you stay with negative people, then you would be like them and would be bearing the bad results of this. But, on the other hand, if you spend your time with positive persons, then you would be having positive attitude towards your problems and would be ready to face them. By this, most of your life's problems would be solved easily.

Don't think too much over situations: If you want to do any work then just go ahead and do it. Do not think about the others' reaction on it. Surely think about the results of it but not too much, lest it should create tensions.

Live in the present: If you are always remembering the past, or dreaming and planning about the future, then you would be losing the happiness of the present. So, it's very important to be always happy and tension free, live in the present and enjoy every moment of it.

Don't undervalue yourself: We often undervalue ourselves when comparing to others. Our attention is always on our weaknesses and we forget our qualities and capabilities. Everyone is special in their own way, that is, some people get profits in business while others get promotions in their jobs. Someone is good in studies and another is good in sports. Some women are quite capable in household activities while some women handle the professional work front efficiently. So, we all are special and we are not inferior to anyone. To have this feeling in our heart, we must have confidence on ourselves and it helps to win over the difficulties. This will make us become tension free and happy.

Art to keep self happy: This is the most important thing. Different people get happiness in different ways. We should leave the habit making other people responsible for our happiness and sorrow. Why should we wait for others making us happy? When we have learned the art to keep ourselves happy, tensions vanish.

Keep walking: The body's cells' receptive power increases while we walk. There is movement in each nerve, so the production of hormones responsible for tension decreases, therefore, the existing tension goes out by your breathing process. That is why doctors and health experts always advise people having depression to walk regularly.

Avoid sedentary life: By sitting for long hours, our body tends towards harmful changes. Although, we may not pay any attention to them. For example, if we sit in front of the TV for a very long time, it is harmful and we can become the victim of many diseases.

Participate in social works: You can give new direction to positive works on the basis of unity that social work develops. Be creative. There is no need to organize high level events for social activities. Even small gestures are effective. Even though if you are working in your garage, there also you can bring the changes. Take care of others' needs while working in a group. You can compromise with their suggestions, unless it is not hurting your ideals.

Adopt new habits to begins: To learn any habit, there is simple way- change of behaviour with experience. It is described as an automatic reaction for special situations, which can be obtained by results of learning and reviewing. When behaviour is developed in such a manner to be automatic, it is said to become a habit. Generally, habits don't need our attention. Habits play an important part in our daily life. We adopt different habits, and they become a part of our life. Habits can be good or bad. Hard work, reading, writing, regular exercise, meditation, etc are good habits. Alcohol, addiction, lethargy, laziness, telling lies, being dishonest, theft, deceiving others, etc are example of bad habits.

1. **Make a good beginning:** Good beginnings are the base of work. The saying goes, "Well Begun is Half Done". So, we should start with a good beginning to learn good habits. We should make strong oaths and have strong inspiration. We should not confuse our mind. For example, one nursing student decided to study for a certain period at a certain time. He should decide timely and then stick to the plan to ensure success.

2. **Develop good habits:** It is important to practise the new habits until they become a part of our daily routine. Beware of delays or disruptions, as they weaken our habit making. For example, we should not give lame excuses like headache, lack of interest, to delay the work.

3. **Choose the favourable climate:** Developing the good habits is also dependent on an energetic atmosphere. For example, one student who wants to work hard, should have the company of hard-working students, not the company of lazy students who are not interested in studies.

4. **Don't stop till your goal achieved:** Once habits form, they should be made stronger. So, this should be continued till it becomes deeply rooted.

By adopting these small efforts, we can lessen our tension and be happy.

Viewpoint for Staying Young

In the whole world, who doesn't want to stay young forever? But, it is not enough to simply desire such a thing, you must have to do a lot of work, so that the aging signs don't reflect. Old age is the eternal truth. But if you don't let it overcome you, then you will feel young forever. Despite being young at heart, it is also important to stay young physically, and this is what we are giving some tips for:

Keep your mind healthy: In the language of psychology, an unhealthy mind is the sign of an unhealthy body. Our will power grows out of a healthy mind. If one has a healthy mind, he can spend a happy life even with an unhealthy body. On the other hand, a person with a healthy body but an unhealthy mind, cries all his life.

Now the thing is how to keep your mind healthy, or at least try your best to achieve this. According to me, the mind can be kept healthy by adopting the following methods :

1. **Learn laughing and making others laugh:** Yes, on laughing, our body produces endorphins and serotonin hormones, which help our body and mind to stay healthy.

2. **Learn to express gratitude:** This is a part of gratitude therapy. When we thank our surrounding things or the persons who have helped us directly or indirectly we achieve mental peace.

3. **Keep a positive attitude:** Negativity encourages negative thoughts and positivity leads to the positive thoughts. A positive viewpoint reduces your tensions, resulting in keeping your mind healthy. Try to stay away from negative people or make them also think positive like you. This also includes not to criticize others.

4. **Keep yourself busy:** It is said that an empty mind is the devil's workshop. Though the mind is never empty but diverts itself to useless things. So, one should keep one's mind busy in useful things.

5. **Read good books and articles:** It is said that you become what you read. So, good reading would give you good thoughts in your mind and keep it healthy.

6. **Keep your enthusiasm high:** It's important to follow logical rules to be successful. The things said by great persons fill us with new enthusiasm by reading them. Only those can have a great personality who don't leave the work incomplete or halfway done, despite several hurdles but keep on trying to work best with the same enthusiasm. Success is directly related to enthusiasm and excitement. The one who learns to keep their enthusiasm and energy alive, will be energetic, and the world is for energetic people. Energetic persons never let their enthusiasm come down, they keep doing the work which scares or challenges them the most. Because, they know that success could be gained by fighting and not getting scared.

Enthusiasm is the scale of human progress and fortune. The one who is enthusiastic, gets progress. Fortune favours the person who works with enthusiasm. Where there is no enthusiasm, no excitement, there is no growth. Nothing grows beneath a cold sheet of ice. No work can be done without enthusiasm. To get the desired results one has to do hard work with enthusiasm. So, start from today with enthusiasm, new hopes, and try to participate in life and turn life into a better experience. So, start being enthusiastic today!

Personal: We need to make some good decisions, and have good thoughts that prevent us from getting any of life's bad experiences. Life has given us everything. But to think everything as one's own is wrong. Because just as life gives us something quickly, it snatches things from us even faster. Many incidents happen in our life about which we wonder, "Why me?" Don't take anything personally. Because if we don't get the things we desire, we feel sad. We should understand that everything has its limitations and can't be extended. Don't take anything very personal and move forward.

Listen to your heart: The decisions taken by the heart could be wrong, but you will never repent for them. When we take decisions with our heart, it's our own decision and not controlled by others. When we work on the task with our heart, we feel happy, so to live a happier life we should take decisions through our heart.

Know the strong side: Our ability to take a strong stand plays an important role to live a good life. Everyone is strong in some way or the other. The main thing is to identify what is that. To live a good life, a person should work with his strong side. If we do take a strong stand, our decisions, thoughts and living style reflect this positivity.

Don't compare: If you are comparing yourself with anyone, you are devaluing yourself. Don't compare yourself with anyone. Compare with yourself only. This will ensure that we should not get tensed, which harms us.

Keep yourself fit: 'Health is wealth', we have heard this so many times and it is very true. If we are not healthy, how could we wish for good long life. A weak person spends more than half of his lifetime visiting doctors and becomes mentally weak. If we are not healthy, we can't do any work wholeheartedly and with enthusiasm.

Do something unique: If anybody does the same work over and over again, he would be bored. The same applies to life. If we live monotonous life, we won't enjoy it. So, do something unique of your choice, which gives you happiness.

Keep yourself happy: It's better to learn more about yourself rather to know the choices. If a person is not happy with himself, then how could he make others happy. To keep yourself happy, spend some time with yourself, understand yourself, and then only you can lead a happy life.

Ever laughing persons stay younger: Your little smile makes others happy and this is beneficial to you also. Everyone has a wish to look younger and beautiful. If you are one of them, start laughing openly. By doing this, your blood circulation gets improved on your whole face which makes you young and beautiful.

❏

Chapter 3

Ikigai from Logotherapy

As every person has some special quality in himself, every country also has one special lifestyle, which keeps on continually developing according to the unique conditions.

Similarly, Japanese lifestyle also developed from Logotherapy and finally culminated in Ikigai.

What is Logotherapy?

Logotherapy means- the good motives to live life. Logotherapy was developed by neurologist and psychologist, Victor Frankl. He based it on the belief that any person's primary inspiration is for searching the meaning of life. (It is described as "the third Viennese school of psychotherapy" with Freud 's psycho analysis and Adler's personal psychology being the other two.)

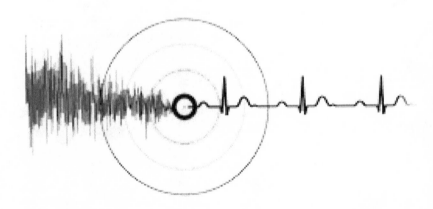

Logotherapy is based on existence analysis which concentrates on the meaning of Kierkegard, which is opposite to Alfred Adler's and Nietzsche's will to power, or Freud's will to pleasure theory. Instead of power or pleasure, Logotherapy is based on the belief that trying to find the meaning of life is the primary and most powerful inspirational power. A brief introduction of this system is given in Frankl's famous book 'Man's Search For Meaning', in which he writes about how his principles helped him to escape from his holocaust experiences, and how that experience further strengthened and developed his principles. At present, there are several Logotherapy institutes all over the world.

The theory of Logotherapy is derived from the Greek word logo (cause). Frankl's theory is based on that any person's primary inspirational power is to search for meaning in life. The following list of principles represent the original theory of logo therapy:"

The meaning of life can be found in every situation, even in pitiable situations also.

Our Main inspiration to live is our will to search for the meaning in life.

What we do, we experience or at least when we are facing continuous pains, in that situation we have the freedom of searching for the meaning of life.

The human soul exists in the context of many different beliefs of Logotherapy. But, the use of the word "soul" is not spiritual or religious. In Frankl's view, the soul is the human's will. So, the thrust is on the search for meaning, which is not necessarily the search for God or any supernatural person. Frankl also noted all the hurdles for humanity in the search for the meaning of life. He warned against "prosperity, pleasure and materialism" in the search for meaning.

Motive in life, meaning in life, building existence, vacuum, and will for meaning, appear in Frankl's writing of Logotherapy, along with those who defined the principles of a positive psychological system. Frankl observed that when someone's search for meaning is obstructed, it could be psychologically harmful for that person. A positive life is joined with motive, meaning, strong beliefs, memberships in groups, dedication for a cause, life values and clear objectives. In adult development and matured principles, motive is included in the idea of life. Maturity emphasizes on the motive of life, directions, and a clear understanding of intentions, which contributes to this feeling that life is worthwhile.

Frankl's thoughts were incorporated into experiments by Crumbaugh and Maholich's "Purpose in Life" (PIL), which estimates the meaning and motive of a person's life. Examining the experiments, they found that, the meaning of life mediates between the relations of religion and welfare, uncontrollable tensions and use of alcoholic substances, depression and self-abuse. Crumbaugh found that Seeking Of Noetic Goals(SONG) test is a supplementary solution of public internet petitions (PIL). When public welfare petitions scales the presence of meaning, SONG measures the inclination towards meaning. One score in public welfare petitions and a high score in SONG will predict better results in application of Logotherapy.

Logo-Medicinal Thoughts and Cure

Control over tensions: Tensions can be controlled by identifying the objective of our situation. About this use of Logotherapy, there are lectures given by Tim Sanders, New York Times writer, in which he tells how he uses this theory to remove the tensions of his fellow airlines passengers by asking them the objectives of their journey. When he does that, his fellow passengers' whole attitude changes, and despite, however, much they may be saddened, they remain happy throughout the journey. Overall, Frankl's belief was that a troubled man cannot understand that his tension is the result of dealing with a feeling of incompetence and lacking of life's meaning.

Cure of Neurosis: Frankl gives the example of two insane disease factors:- Over-determination --one strong idea of any point which makes its end unreachable. Over imaginative reflections ---more attention towards oneself which tries to escape from neurosis which he thinks is predecided. To remove expected tensions and to cure the resultant neurosis, Logotherapy gives paradoxical intentions, in which the patient wants to do the opposite of his most wanted motive.

One person, who is scared (meaning someone who feels the tension in advance), does not get good sleep, will try very hard to sleep (meaning thinking over ideas), and this will put hurdles for their capabilities to do this. A logo therapist will recommend that he should go to bed and try to sleep. He will remove his, already present, tensions which kept him awake. This way, he was allowed to sleep for the expected time.

Depression: Viktor E. Frankl believed that depression is of a psychological, physical and spiritual level. On the psychological level, he believed that insufficient feelings arise from the working beyond capabilities. On the physical level he validated important lows which he defined as the scarcity of physical energy. In the end, Frankl believed that on the spiritual level, sad people have to face tensions of who they are, and what they should be in this context. Frankl advises if motive seems unapproachable, then the person loses the future feeling and this way it leads to depression. This way Logotherapy's motive is "to change the patient's viewpoint towards life as a work along with disease."

Compulsive Obsessive Disorder (COD)

Frankl believed that people suffering from an obsessive-compulsive disorder are devoid of a feeling of perfection which most other people have. Doctors should concentrate on changing their neurotic viewpoint towards neurosis instead of concentrating on fighting repeated thoughts or repeated works or changing the personal signs of disease. So, it is important to identify that the patient "is not responsible for his obsessive thoughts" but "surely he is responsible for his views towards these thoughts". Frankl advised that it is important to identify the patient's inclination towards perfection. It should be learned in the form of fortune, and also accept some points of uncertainty. Lastly, people should ignore their obsessive thoughts on the basis of Logotherapy, and should search for the meaning of life despite these thoughts.

A type of mental disorder: Though the Logotherapy's objective was not to deal with serious disorders, Frankl believed that Logotherapy could benefit the people suffering from schizophrenia. He identified the roots of schizophrenia in physical lethargy. In this disease, the patient, suffering from schizophrenia, thinks of himself as an object instead a subject. Frankl advised that a person suffering from schizophrenia could be taught firstly to ignore the sounds and continually stop himself. In the review period, the schizophrenic person should be taken towards positive activities, because "even for schizophrenic people the fortune and freedom remains for that disease, which humans always have, however sick he may be, in every situation and every moment of life, till the last moment."

What does Ikigai do?

As you have been told before, that the Japanese people have developed the theory of Ikigai from Logotherapy. In the

Japanese language, there is a very short but deep meaning of the word "Ikigai". "Iki" means life, and "gai" means the price or value. This way, Ikigai means 'the value of life or the reason to stay alive'. In Japan, it is seen in a different way. There are people who believe that the other person cannot decide this value for your life. You will have to decide yourself what the value of your life is. It would be possible only when you would understand why are you alive?

Most of the people among us have questions in their mind, like how much more money do we need to earn for living our life nicely? Which things do we need to get to feel satisfied? Which hobby to fulfil so that our relatives and friends will envy us? Among these questions, there is Ikigai, which asks you: "Do you know, why are you alive?" Only for your bank balance? Or for a duplex or for a four BHK? To pay the premium? Just think and tell us, what is the password for your happy life?

Ikigai says that people's viewpoint to see life is changing. It has happened before, but people's feelings are in the limelight in the 21st century. This is the thinking that goes beyond money. Money is not everything. Think beyond this. Think by yourself and see why are you living? Money in your account, a house in a posh colony, a shining car at your doorstep, by thinking all these factors all the time, are you not wasting your real life? What is the value of your life, if life doesn't exist? By joining your social identity—which is connected to your work, and your personal identity—which is your life's rating—you reach the point which is aimed at by Ikigai. Whatever and whenever you do, whether it is office work, your business or to fulfil your hobby, friendship, social work or roaming around, it is getting deposited in the credit score of your Ikigai.

According to the Japanese every person has one Ikigai. In Japanese, Ikigai means the cause of your waking up in the morning. It is called the motive of life or the cause of enjoying the life also.

The area inside the cutting circle each other is your Ikigai. If there is scarcity in the things written inside the circles of life, then you are not living life with perfection. Not only to this, the scarcity could affect your wishes for long and happy life.

Have You Found Your Ikigai?

- What work are you going to do, which you like to do?
- Is it a work that will benefit the world?
- Are you an expert in the work which you are going to do?
- Is it the work in which you could earn money?
- What could you do to live a long, healthy and happy life?"

"Kabhi Kisi Ko Mukkammal Jahan Nahin Milta,
Kabhi Zameen To Kabhi Aasman Nahin Milta"

These lines of a ghazal come true for the life situations of any professional. There will always remain some aspects of life which will make people unhappy. If they are getting good money, they may not like the work. If they do the work of their liking, then they struggle with the money aspects. If the work and money is good, then they may not have the spare time to spend with family. If they are getting everything, still there may be something pinching them and they may not have fulfilled something. Ikigai is the passion for which people start doing their work, for waking up in the morning, willingly or unwillingly.

But, does one find out what one's passion is? I have asked this question to myself and other people known to me. Earlier, I thought that only the new generation (born after 1990), is exciting about this. But, this is not true. After I saw some research works which tell that my generation people (born between 1970-1980) also think about making a career in the field of their passion.

Mostly people think that the thought of searching for one's own passion in work has come from Western countries, but it's not true. We learned before that Ikigai is a Japanese word and there are similar thoughts available in different cultures. I have already explained through diagrams and am again repeating that anything should have the following four things compulsorily in it to be Ikigai :

- thing you love.
- thing you are an expert in doing.
- what the world needs. And,
- thing which will earn you money.

So, in your case whatever activities fulfil the above four things, you could call that your Ikigai. In my case, translation and blogging are my Ikigai which fulfil the above four things.

Find the motive in which you deeply believe: The people can search for their passion or Ikigai in different ways. Any life changing good and bad experiences, deep internal discussion, a sudden event which changes your life's direction could introduce a motive of life. To search for the strong motive, which you care for, will keep you honest with yourself, and you will be focused even in difficult situations. You can ask yourself one question in starting your search for your purpose. The question is "What changes would I like to see in the world?"

Stop thinking start working: If you are a person of many passions or waiting for the right moment then you should know that there is no age to follow your passion. Mark Zuckerberg founded Facebook at the age of 19, while on the other hand, Charles Flint founded IBM at the age of 61. True passion could be identified by trying again and again or being unsuccessful several times. In this journey, every step is important which takes you toward your goal. I would like to advise you that if you follow too many passions, then you should cut down your list to the top two passions. Then follow those two with all of your heart and decide what do you want to do finally.

Be in contact with people of the same passion: Keep contact with those people who have the same passions and hobbies as you. Meet those people also who have tried your passions. By meeting such people, you will know each other's thoughts and get a chance to work together. You can learn from their mistakes and they would also tell you about their mistakes. In contrast, if you work alone then making your presence felt would not be impossible, but very difficult. When the people of the same passion work together, then it becomes a healthy competition. So, it becomes easier to identify talented people.

Don't be disturbed with hurdles on the road: When listening to his heart, a person decides to follow his passion or Ikigai, then there are hurdles on the unknown roads. He doesn't get the persons to walk with him. There is no guide also. People laugh at him, calling his thoughts useless and illogical. It all happened with Alibaba company's founder Jack Ma. He took all these hurdles and obstacles as challenges. He fell down several times and every time he got up, he dusted himself and kept walking. What could be any other alternative?

Identify your passion or Ikigai. Not only following it, but searching for it could be your life's important journey towards self-confidence. This journey would be full of thorns and challenges. There would be ups and downs, and bad weather in your way. You have to keep confidence in your heart and you should know that big journeys are not completed in one night. You can't wait sitting on your easy chair that someone would give you keys to your golden future. You have to get up, walk and do not stop until you reach your destination.

Chapter 4

The Search for Flow

Nobody has leisure time in this topsy-turvey of daily life. If anyone gets a little time, then they waste it just like that. They don't put this time in the right work. If we want to make our life better then, we would have to use the leisure time better. We can give good direction to our life in this time.

If you are a working person, then you can do some better work for yourself or for your family in your spare time. You can take the best time out for everyone. By this, you would be everyone's favourite and your time will be utilised.

It's very difficult question-- what to do in your free time or spare time. So, today Hindivaani will tell you how to utilise your free time? So, how is your free time being used? Because every moment is precious for human.

We all learn to postpone our today's work for tomorrow by blaming others for our mistakes. Although, we should not postpone any of today's work for tomorrow, because by keep on postponing the work then there would be too much work accumulated for you. If you don't do the work today, then you won't be able to do it tomorrow also, as there will be tomorrow's works also to catch up with. For example, you don't want to eat stale food after you have seen fresh food being served. The same applies to work.

Time is always on the move; you can't make jewellery out of it and keep it. Nobody owns or controls the time. But time can be well used and be kept like jewellery, or else it would be destroyed. The optimum use of time is more important than use of money, because money also depends on time.

Time is the key to success. If you want to be successful in life, then you have to move with time in every step. The wheel of time is moving very fast. You and I might be sleeping but time is moving with its regular speed. You must have seen written at many places "Time, death and the customer don't wait for anyone." Often, we hear from someone that what can they do, there is no time. But in reality, this is not so. In this world, everyone has the same 24 hours. Time doesn't wait for us, we have to manage the time.

One day and night have 24 hours. This means $24 \times 60 \times 60 = 86,400$ seconds. God credits 86,400 seconds into every creature's account every day. Even then, humans cry about shortage of time. You will be surprised to know the reason, it is that you are spending your time without thinking or planning. If we spend time wisely, then we would have enough time for all the works we plan. If someone's progress and development is halted, it means he is playing with time. On the road to development, the biggest enemy is the wastage of time. Bygone time doesn't come back. So, make a habit, to move with time.

- Galileo used to sell the medicines. He invented many scientific things.
- The bad news is that time is running out, however, the good news is that you are the pilot of it.
- Take care of the minutes, and the hours will take care of themselves.
- You can be late but the time will not wait.
- Whatever things are there in the world, all contain time in it.
- There are no more precious things in this world than time.
- Ishwar Chandra Vidyasagar was so punctual about time, that whenever he used to go college, the shopkeepers of the path used to correct their watches by seeing him.
- The person who makes good use of time, and doesn't waste a single moment, is very fortunate and achieve big.

Stage of getting Flow

Franklin has said - "Don't waste time, because life is made of time."

The needle of time is the building material of the palace of life. Nature hasn't made anybody rich or poor, he has distributed his precious wealth equally. Labour goes to waste if work is not done on time. So, make a habit to do your work on time. For example, if the bread isn't turned on the pan in time, it will get burnt and its place is in the dustbin. Similarly, you should change yourself according to time, otherwise, your condition would be like burnt bread. Every moment of time comes with the possibility of a bright future. Who knows the moment we are wasting thinking useless thoughts, it could be our moment of fortune and success.

Should Know, What to Do

The first step is to decide the goals for earning any success in life. Setting the goal is an activity for which you need to give sufficient time, and this is the proper use of time. Because once you set your goal then you can start trying to achieve it and be able to concentrate in a better way by trying.

What to do to Achieve The Goal?

What is important to achieve your goals? Dreaming about achieving the goal is definitely beautiful but it's also very important to know what to do to achieve them. You start from some point and that's your starting point. When you are at some special time, and you start your first step from there towards your set goal. It is very important to know what is important to make your journey successful towards your goal. You should make favourable attempts to achieve your goals and your efforts should be according to your goals.

Setting the goal: To set the goal is the very first and important necessity, and if your attempts are temporary, and you are not serious about what you are going to do, then probably you haven't set any goals for yourself or perhaps your goals are not clear. So, first of all, set your goals. You go to school daily except on holidays, but you need to set the goals for better studies. How much trouble do you take for going to school, then why can't you study well? To set the goal is very important, be it getting education, or any activities related to sports. Similarly, if you are a professional then you need to set the goal to reach on the top in business, because practicing the setting of goals makes you serious for achieving them.

How to set goals: Be clear about your goals. What is your goal? Is it only reaching school, or reaching school on time? It makes all the difference. Your results, whatever goal you have set, would be accordingly. If you are questioned for reaching late to school, so it might be so because you hadn't set the goal for reaching school in time. So, be clear about your goals and set meaningful goals for yourself.

Then you will have to identify those of your goals which you are trying to achieve consciously or unconsciously, in both ways. If you are aware about your goals and they are clear, then you can correctly describe your attempts to get the goals. So, you have to set the goals after much thoughts and then try to achieve them.

You can have more than one goal: Every time you have many big or small goals and you can find out about them any time. These goals could be instant, short term or medium term or for a long time or might be even lifelong. For example, to reach office on time, could be your instant goal.

If you need to finish your work and you have to submit it to school, college or office within two days, then this is your short-term goal.

In the same way, if you want to achieve your goal in office for one financial year, this is your medium-term goal. Similarly, to finish your syllabus for the annual examination in school or college could be your medium-term goal.

Along with this, you can set your goal to be successful in business in the long term, or to finish your studies and after that becoming a professional architect could be your long-term goal. It could be possible that you might have set the goal to establish a charitable hospital for the needy. Likewise, generally your goal could be to become a good, religious and cheerful person for the society.

You give importance to each of your goals and you want to achieve all the goals in a certain time. Is this right? The following are a few methods which will help you to decide your goal and to achieve them:

Be practical: Adopt a practical attitude towards the goals you have set. This means you will have to be practical about your attempts for deciding the goals and to achieve them. If you set a goal which probably you cannot achieve, then what is the use of such goal? If you decide such a goal which needs lots of resources, which probably you don't have, then what is the meaning of such a goal? If you are lacking in physical strength, patience and health, and still you set the goal to become an athlete, you won't be much successful. Surely, you can try to improve your health and strength, but if it's not possible then you should avoid setting such goals.

Listen to and follow your heart: For deciding your goal, listen to your heart and follow it. For example, it might be possible that you want to expand your business, not for profit, but for social welfare causes. Follow what you want to do. It's not important that you should do everything for profit. If you feel that your responsibilities are not for earning more profits but social welfare, then do it. And move ahead in that direction because you will be much happier.

Equally, it might be that you don't have any interest in adopting the medical field as a career, though people will keep telling you the benefits of being a professional doctor. Similarly, you might be pressurised for joining the family business. Don't decide under the pressure of friends, family members or others. Choose the career of your choice—because, after all, you will have to work, according to this career, for your livelihood lifelong. So, wouldn't you like to choose the career which you like and you will be feeling happy doing that work. Surely, you want to do this. And in reality, to really choose what you want to do, you need a lot of courage.

How to achieve different goals in life: One should set the goals fearlessly and start the attempts to get it with full courage. All the great goals are achieved by those people who started small, beginning in an ordinary way. If you have excitement in yourself to get your goals, then it's not difficult to attain any goals.

To accomplish the goals sacrifices are necessary. You will have to be courageous to achieve your goals, be they small or big.

If your friends are compelling you to spend time on Whatsapp with them, or inviting you for late night parties, then for the sake of goal achievements, you will have to refuse them. Your time is precious and if you would party late into the night, obviously you won't wake up fresh in the morning. And you will be reaching late to your school, college or workplace. If your goal is to reach everywhere on time, then you would have to say no courageously to useless and unnecessary activities.

For example, if you have to follow a certain type of diet to achieve the goal, then you will have to be committed for it. It would be in your favour if you follow the diet plan for your goal, then only you would be achieving your goal. Isn't that right? Then why are you repenting in doing this?

You should be ready to leave anything which is an obstacle in your path towards achieving goals and have enough courage for it. Your courage only will make sure of success in goal achieving. To achieve the goals successfully, you should keep following points in mind.

Time is precious: If you set the time for your goal-achieving, then you should follow it cautiously.

Time is precious as it goes away very fast. Bygone time doesn't come back. So, you should escape from those activities which are obstacles for your goals.

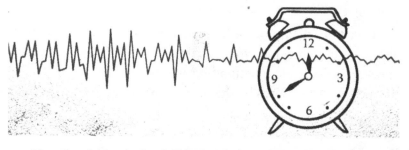

You should have the full information about the time you are spending on any activity. This will help you in time management for any work. So, you will have to be actively trying to save the time. You should pay attention to time management for goal achievements. Remember, it is always very important to reach on time everywhere.

Persistence is necessary for time saving: Be persistent for your goals and attempts to getting them. If you show a little carelessness or emotion then your attempts will slowdown, and you would miss the goal.

If you really want to achieve the goals then attempt in the right direction. If you keep changing your thinking and setting several goals then you are not persistent in one goal. Then you won't get any single goal. In this way, you would have wasted both your time and energy, getting nothing. So, you should use your time and energy wisely, make sure you have both in abundance.

So, spend your time wisely, and decide your goal very seriously and thoughtfully. You should decide your goals after studying the loss and profit thoroughly. Besides you should be quite clever in achieving the goals.

If you are serious for reaching your goals, then stay serious for your attempt in the right direction. Besides, persistence is also necessary, and if you work regularly and with total commitment, definitely you will be successful. Also, you will be successful in managing your time and resources.

Don't get disappointed, boost yourself: If you are serious about your achieving your goals, then you should not be dependent upon the encouraging words of others, nor should you be weakened down by the hurdles in the way that have been put by others and their negative activities. Actually, you should try with more self-confidence rather than being disappointed. Be happy while setting your goals and stay cheerful attempting for your goals achievements. If you work hard to reach your goals but you are not happy, then there won't be any results of your attempts. Mental happiness makes you capable and increases the quality of your attempts.

And in this way, you won't feel your attempts as a burden but they will be useful for you. Even if you don't get success soon, don't turn back from your goals, and keep trying for achievements. Set your goals and definitely you can get it. If you are not successful in the first attempt, try again and again. You must have heard that "Failure is the first milestone in the path of success." If you have failed in the first attempt then it clears many aspects of the attempts done by you. And you would improve them and make your attempts more meaningful and productive.

Suffering from a disturbed mind: If our mind is disturbed, then we can sit in solitude and try to calm down our mind. It makes our mind calm. You can listen to music. There could be many reasons for a disturbed mind, it is quite necessary to identify and remove it. For example, there could be irritation due to lack of sleep, so take full & sound sleep for 6-7 hrs.

Your body remains fit and healthy by taking care of your diet. It helps to keep your mind healthy. If you feel too much disturbed, you could do meditation. Meditation is very beneficial making your mind to calm down.

You can go to some serene places to calm your mind. Do the things which give you pleasure. You could take some time out for yourself from this rushing world. By this, your mind remains happy. Waking up early in the morning and going for a walk is very good for health and mind. To breathe in fresh air has so many advantages.

If we take some decisions with a disturbed mind, we can't differentiate between right or wrong. Mostly people between 16 to 25 years of age have unstable and disturbed mind. They make a lot of mistakes and lost in the mesh. They take wrong decisions in haste. Sometimes, it is possible to correct them, but at other times it is impossible. Hasty talks and decisions happen with a disturbed mind along with, age also matters. Decisions taken with stable minds are possibly more correct. Our mind gets stable with growing age. But at a younger age also, people doing work with a calm mind achieve much. Right decisions could get you to the right destination in your life. People with a calm mind have talent in society, with whom people want to connect.

In my view, it is very important to have a calm mind. We can't do any right thing with a disturbed mind. Life is not the gamble which could be left to destiny. You have to move it with your mind, brain and thoughts. For living a good life, a healthy body and healthy mind is necessary. It is important to take care of both.

Physical health is more important than mental health. The mind feels happiness when the body is fit. Though our mind gets disturbed due to external conditions, even then our physical health helps to calm it down. So, physical health has great importance.

If we feel agitated, and the body is also weak, then it won't be easy to go out or make any other efforts to calm down. But if the body is healthy, then we can do many things to calm ourselves. So, keep yourself fit and healthy for mental health.

Why Simple Living?

The intelligent people of Japan have followed this saying and made a place for themselves in history. Sant Kabirdas, Mahatma Gandhi, Pope Francis, and Abraham Lincoln are some of these people. All these people have lived their life very simply, and have inspired many people around them.

Very few people live an ordinary life. Some want to fulfil their wishes, some want to impress others with their wealth. Here it is told why one should live simply:

Closer to family: When you leave living artificial life, where you always try to impress others, and move ahead for a simple life, you come closer to your culture. By this, you become closer to your family members. The love given by them makes you happy.

Identify yourself: When you stop searching for more and more things to satisfy yourself and spend more time with yourself, you finally identify with who you are in real life.

Feeling of control: When you live a simple life, you need minimum requirements. When you don't have any loan on your head for buying things, you feel more confident. And because of this, you don't need to earn more money for paying bills and debts. You don't need to be too busy in work. You have a feeling of control in life.

Lower level of tension: You are not under pressure for earning more money in comparison to your siblings, friends, neighbours. Now you won't want more bank balance, bigger house, a bigger car to feel good about yourself. When you choose the simple living, all the tension would go away.

Balanced life: Now you don't have to work hard to reach at the top, The reasons for this is that now your desires would be limited and you can fulfil them easily. Even if the income is good. This way you will reach home in time and spend time with family. It helps in balancing your life.

Chapter 5

Longevity Masters

Japanese people are more fit and healthy in comparison to people of other countries. They remain active for their work throughout their life. How healthy the Japanese people are, you can guess with the fact that the world's oldest people are in Japan. Japan is such a country where men's life average is 80 years, and women die after the average of 86 years. This means in total, Japanese people live to the longest age. What's the secret of Japanese people's living a long life? Come, let's raise the curtain over this secret.

From Japan to America, in many countries' culture, a healthy life in old age is directly connected with objective lifestyle. But till now, it was believed that life with motive is more beneficial for aged adults rather than young people. Hill says that it doesn't matter in which age a person decides his goals? The results of past studies show that in people living for motive, the death rate's risk is much less, which means that life expectancy increases.

Come, Let's Know the Secret of the Longevity of The Japanese

Every person desires a long life. Longevity's blessing is always included in the elders' blessings, and we try so much for a long and healthy life. But you will be surprised that there is

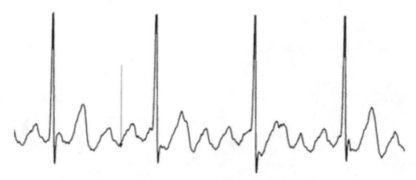

one country of the world where people do have longevity. This country's name is Japan, where women's average age is 86 years and men's average age is 80 years.

Not only this, the number of 100-year-old Japanese is no less. In this case, it is natural to think about what methods the Japanese could have adopted so that they get this long and healthy life. Let's know the secret of Japanese people's longevity.

It is known by the recent studies that the Japanese people's diet is the cause of their longevity. And as you know, a nutritious diet can give you longevity along with making your health better.

The Japanese give importance to nutrition in their diet and they use grains, vegetables, fruits, meat, and fish in their diet. In the food of the Japanese people, green vegetables and lentils are very important. And, they use these in surplus. Lentils and green vegetables are full of antioxidants and photo-chemicals which save us from cancer and heart diseases.

To keep their food full of nutrients, Japanese people never eat more than their hunger, Japanese people always eat a little less than their hunger instead of overeating. They prefer to eat fish rather than red meat, because the vitamins and oil of fish help the body to become internally stronger.

There is one more speciality of the Japanese which makes them fit. They don't like to sit idle even in the age of 60 years.

They like to do something and keep themselves busy all the time.

To keep themselves busy for fitness, the Japanese pay special attention to medicine. These people like to be cured with natural ayurveda medicines rather than allopathic medicines, because of which they are saved from the chemicals present in allopathic medicine. As you know how harmful addictive substances are, and the Japanese people stay away from cigarettes and alcohol, so that they should not suffer any loss.

The Japanese know very well how to laugh heartily and live life openly. And the immune system of the Japanese remains stronger. They face any adverse situations with a calm mind rather than taking tensions.

Exercise has very important role for a healthy body, and this habit is given to the Japanese at a very early age. Because of this, exercise is an inseparable part of their daily routine.

In Japan, special attention is given to cleanliness, besides diet and exercise for the good health and longevity. Here, the books returned to the library are cleaned with UV techniques, so that harmful germs should not infect others.

The secret of the longevity of the Japanese is connected to their lifestyle. Every work of the Japanese is related to their lifestyle. Giving importance to nutritious diets, exercise, and cleanliness the Japanese keep the attitude of living life in a smiling manner. And, this is the reason of their long and healthy life.

Use of eastern herbs: The Japanese use eastern herbs and do not depend on allopathic medicines.

Eating fish instead of red meat: Here people eat fish in place of red meat, so there is no deficiency of nutrients in their bodies. They get oil, vitamins and nutrients from fish. They don't eat red meat which is full of bad fats which cause an increasing cholesterol level. By doing this, they don't suffer from heart diseases.

Keep cleanliness: Japan is considered one of the cleanest countries of the world. The Japanese prevent themselves from contagious diseases by taking extra care. Even the books returned in library are cleaned with UV techniques.

Using lots of green vegetables: In the Japanese plate, half the plate is full of green vegetables. Besides this, they eat

different types of lentils. The Japanese like very much to eat mixed vegetable salad. That is why because of antioxidants and photochemicals they don't get heart diseases and cancer.

Do exercise daily: Every house has a rule that they have to go to do yoga, karate, and martial arts compulsorily. By doing these exercises, their mind remains calm and the body keeps fit. They don't leave it even in old age.

Eat less than hunger: When the Japanese have their stomach 4/5 filled, they stop eating. They like to eat less and never overfill their stomach. It is seen in studies that by doing this their aging decreases.

Remain active for a long time: There is no retirement age in Japan. They like to work even after crossing the age of 60 years. They don't like to sit idle or sleeping, so they keep themselves busy.

Live life fully: They know how to live happily even in adverse conditions. They like to spend their life away from useless tensions and fighting. They do social work and help people because they believe their life has some motive.

Stay away from bad habits: Smoking, alcohol, salty foods, over eating, etc are bad habits that are not included in their daily routine, so they live longer.

Laugh heartily: Laughing heartily is a medicine, so body ache and depression get removed. Our immune system gets stronger by laughing, so, they don't forget to laugh at any occasion. They laugh daily for 15 minutes. Your average age increases by 8 years by laughing.

The Japanese like to live social life: The fact about the Japanese that is to be liked is their social unity. The Japanese give priority to collective needs rather than personal needs. "When there is life is short for love, hatred should not be given place in

the heart." And forgive other's mistakes. Having a big heart, "we should forgive those whom we can't forget, and the people whom we can't forgive, we should forget them". We should try to make others happy because if everyone is happy, we will be happier."

Enjoy every moment: Enjoyment is a situation. Most of the time, it depends on yourself. While it's true that we could be less or more fortunate, to be happy is always subjective to mood

Ikigai ✍ 61

and attitude towards life. So, whenever, there is a question of happiness then we have to learn how to do it and have to enjoy fully every day.

Let's see some tips and tricks which help us to be happy, because it can be learned how to be happy. Today, we know very well that happiness depends on us, and not on the uncontrollable outer causes.

How to choose and see to be happy: The first step should be clear to us that we should choose to be happy. Be happy every day, as this is definitely an option. And in the circumstances in which we live, it is an option. Should we believe it or not. There are many things which we can't control, but it doesn't mean that we can't decide to be happy. We can enjoy whatever we have. Now, while it's a viewpoint to be happy with anything, for this we have to do some work on our part. It doesn't show overnight and we won't be ready to be happy ever. It's very important to know the points how to stay happy and practice those points.

Rest and know you can't control everything: The person trying to control everything creates negativity. Because, in this life, to control everything, is impossible. We should know that certain things are not in our hand and give right importance to things. It is important to relate with things. Because sometimes we worry a lot about those things which are no longer important. For this reason, we should learn to rest and accept that there are certain things beyond our reach.

Live in the present: We almost do think and worry about the past things and the things which can't happen. Now, it's important to pay attention to the present. Bygone times can't be returned. The things which can't be changed, are not worthy to worry about. The people living in the present are the happiest people, because they know the time passes very fast. They take advantage of the present time.

Take care: Caring of the body is one of the best tips to be happy. Because it gives us self-respect and welfare. One of the best things to benefit us is to play. Do your regular exercises daily. It is good not only for our body, but it also gives a positive effect on the mind, because it produces endorphin hormones, when improves mental work and helps us to be happy.

Keep positive people around yourself: Sometimes we feel that people around us influence our normal mood. If we surround ourselves with positive and happy persons then we would feel ourselves happier and more positive. This is a fact, so we would have to think about the toxic people and the people who keep us happy. This is not about the leaving the persons aside but we might be surrendering ourselves with people who bring happiness and try to change the mood of the people.

Learn forgiveness: There is no meaning of happiness in good times. The things which happened earlier are not a part of the life now. We should learn to forgive. It is very important that we should forgive and let it go whatever is not good for us.

The world needs happy people. Then why shouldn't we be the first such persons who knows every moment happily. Come, tell yourself and decide that happiness is in my hands.

If world doubts your power, don't be upset. Because gold's purity is always doubted but not of the iron's.

Don't pay attention to those who trouble you. Spend time with those who make you happy.

Our biggest happiness is to do that work which people say you can't do.

Life is very strange. In sad times, one can't sleep and in happier times no one wants to sleep.

Look at yourself in the mirror, find out what do you like most, and consider that.

Give importance to everyone in life, good people will give happiness, bad people will give you lessons.

Search for helpful and great thinking people.

The cause of your sorrow is only you. Change yourself, you will be starting getting happy.

Choose a bouquet of flowers and keep it inside your home near the door.

Learn to forgive everyone, especially yourself.

Wear your favourite clothes.

Happiness is good what you can hold. Overflowing happiness gets jinxed.

Remember, there were mornings when we used to wake up smiling, but now it gets to evening without smiling.

Life is very short. Don't waste it by being sad. However, learn to be happy.

Don't pay attention to bad things and bad people.

Life's best and biggest happiness is imprisoned in our small moments which can only be freed by you.

Pick up the phone and talk to those whom you haven't spoken to for a long time. Really, you will get the happiness which can't be described.

There are lots of people deceiving you in life but there will always be opportunities. You can learn to be happy in such opportunities.

Keep doing your work. Keep busy and don't have free time so you don't have time to feel sad.

Trust in yourself that you could do anything.

Give happiness to people. By doing this, you also learn to be happy.

Think that, there is only today to live, and don't waste it. Determine only to stay happy like it is a religion.

Spend time with inspirational people. Or read about such persons who inspire you.

Getting saddened by others' happiness will not help reduce your bad time, so don't do it.

The persons whom you love, go and tell them now that you love them, and you will be happy without any reason.

Take positive steps towards your destination.

Look at the things which make you happy.

Tell or sing whatever makes you happy.

Touch the things which make you happy like trees, a velvety cat, etc.

Spend time with your good friends.

You can't collect happiness by staying worried about tomorrow. Tomorrow is uncertain. It may be or not. There is only the present you have right now, so be happy today.

Do something which you haven't done so far, but have always wanted to do. You won't have time to be sad.

There will be such a time, when you won't have even time to be sad, so whatever time you have learn to be happy in it.

Teach yourself to stay with positive persons.

Don't get upset with others' talks.

Close your eyes and pay attention to positive things.

Change your habits.

Spend time with children.

Get up every morning and decide "I have to be happy today."

Don't worry about anything.

If you worry, it destroys your body and mind. If you keep thinking, then the mind and intelligence develop. When humans face the situations of their surroundings then there could be two things- struggle or retreat. Auto activities of body especially prepare the body to deal with this situation, which leads to high blood pressure, faster heartbeats, and tensed muscles. The word tension started in medical science in 1940.

There are so many possibilities in the word "tomorrow". Human nature is such that they want happiness, peace, prosperity and success, but these cannot be attained easily in this modern time. Some problems of life have no solution, but some are not as difficult as they seem. Mental exercises solve every problem. It is normal that tense situations may arise sometimes, but if the mental and bodily situations continue like this, then our body parts become weak. Wotton Temple has correctly commented on human life that "humans are born crying, live complaining, and finally die frustrated." The people who live in the present, enjoy the true life. Because bygones are bygones, whatever it was, sad or happy, now has no importance.

Tips to Rescue

We have so many patients who are always in tension because of so many reasons. Some of them are so much in tension that their problems grow even after meeting psychologists and taking medicine. By doing this, not just the person, but the whole family gets troubled. In some cases, the families break down because of these family tensions.

In these cases, some tips are given after consultation along with proper treatment. Out of them, few are very ordinary but very powerful and successful tips which were beneficial for many patients are as follows:

1. First look at the positive side of everything. Trust that whatever is happening in our life is for us.

2. Set your target and make a proper plan to achieve them. Don't live in dreams. Don't have much expectations, not with others nor with your own self. Everyone makes mistakes, so don't take it to your heart.

3. Stay away from negative persons. There could be many meanings of anything. Adopt whatever is good out of them and leave the rest.

4. Laugh heartily. Take any sarcasm on yourself as a joke only. Don't take things too seriously.

5. Walk for 2-3 kilometres daily. And exercise for 20-25 minutes daily.

6. Stay away from junk ot fast food like chowmein, burger, pizza, etc.

7. Acid fruits and water content more in your food.

8. Fulfill your hobbies like listening music, gardening, painting, driving, swimming, etc.

9. Share household and outside work. Don't get stubborn to insist to do all by yourself.

10. Remember, you can't make everyone happy. Do the right work and if someone is not happy, don't worry. Gradually everyone will understand.

11. Every work has to be done faster. But if you give 5 more minutes to it, there won't be any haste to do work.

12. Every day enjoy looking at the nature for 10 minutes. This the gift of God. Clouds in the sky, cold winds, blooming flowers, chirping birds, and playing squirrels all are made for you.

13. Stop thinking of yourself as a victim.

Good Habits

To be successful in life only hard work is not enough, it also depends on how smartly you are working. We all want to be successful. But most of us waste our time in the wrong field. So, with simple habits and thinking smartly you can take your success to a higher level. Good habits are very important for our life. We are taught good habits early in our childhood, and they remain with us lifelong. In the following part, we will try to know the different aspects of good habits related to three different word limits.

These are as follows:

1. **Early Rising:** The Morning time is very beneficial. Your mind and body, both are fresh. You are getting ready for the long day ahead. Don't start your day from office, but start two hours earlier. Decide your targets. Make a list of your To-Do list and make sure you follow it.

2. **Regular Exercise:** For a healthy life, it is necessary to have a healthy body. By doing this you can achieve your target. Exercise daily so your body gets stronger which is necessary to get success.

3. **Get yourself ready:** If your self confidence is high, you win half the battle. If you look good then your self-confidence will be high. The world will see you differently.

4. **Eating right:** Your diet should be such to compel you to move ahead, and not to sleep. If after lunch you will get lethargic and sleepy, it means you have to change your eating habits. Eat light and nutritious food.

Take Care of Your Friendship

Friendship is a very different relation. Friends always help in good or bad times. Have you noticed what type of friend are you for your friends? If not, let us know what is lacking.

It happens in every relation but it is most applicable in friendship. If your friend gets some happiness in life, you also feel happy for him. So, you are eligible to be a good friend. But if you are jealous then you will have to work hard to be a good friend.

It's supposed to be a good quality but it's quite necessary in friendship. Because, there is no formality between friends, and mostly because we want to share our happiness with friends. But you have to understand that friends are also human and need someone to share their feelings with. So, a good friend is such a person who listens to a friend's problems, understand it and support it. Besides this, a good friend is such who shows us our faults in the mirror.

Always stay positive. If you are positive, your friends would feel great. It is saying that good company affects our life deeply. Good company makes one's character. So, we should choose such friends who play a positive role in our character building. In bad company, we can create problems for ourselves and our family.

Rules of Friendship

1. Don't be a victim of misunderstandings about small things.

2. Don't take wrong decision emotionally. Talk openly with your friends.

3. Try to know in which conditions your friend made you angry.

4. Never break the trust of your friend.

5. Don't try to be friendly with the friends of your friend.

6. Everyone makes mistakes. Try to ignore them and forgive each other and promise not to repeat them.

7. Don't give importance to small things.

8. Sometimes friendship break on minor issues like "He didn't SMS me", "He didn't wish me", "Didn't give me notes", "Refused to do my work". Stay away from these.

9. People can't digest others' good friendship. Don't trust others for your friendship.

10. Understand each other. Understanding is the key of good friendship.

Learn to Live

Life is very pleasant, but might be possible you couldn't able to understand the ways of living. How you live your life totally depends on you. To choose the right alternatives is the right way to searching the true meaning of happiness and life. Often, we think of moving ahead in life but never do. If we want to fulfil our dreams by moving ahead, then we would have to get ready for adopting the coming changes of life.

1. I can't control the incidents happening in my life every day, but how I react to them is in my control. So, always remember, incidents are always beyond our power but to manage them is in our hands. This is my power and I would have to adopt it.

2. We have to understand that world is ever-changing. So, my life and world will keep on changing. Whether we adopt these changes or not, they will happen. It would be better to adopt the changes. Accepting these changes would give you happiness. Often some incidents happen in our life that make us frustrated and hopeless. Always remember that life is a long journey. So, we must move ahead and adopt the changes. There will be new experiences. There will be many opportunities to do so much more.

3. Every person wants to progress in life. But for that we would have to come out of our comfort zone, which seems very hard. Sitting at one place, living in one kind of circumstances takes our future into darkness. So, always should come forward and face the situation and change yourself with time. Circumstances will be changed.

4. Always remember that bygone time won't ever come back. But the coming time could be made beautiful. So, come forward. Accept new challenges. The difficult present time will encourage us because it looks forward to a beautiful future.

5. The persons who can't leave their most negative habits lag behind. We always are attached to old, sad and negative memories. So, we bear the pains every moment. It doesn't make difference to anybody else. Forgiving past things, pick up the pen of the present and write your future for the making of a golden future.

6. We have a creative power inside us to wish to do something new. Positive thinking grows. We get power to face the situations. There would be new life experiences. Our thoughts change by accepting new challenges successfully. We get new thoughts and search for new ways. Always remember whenever we move forward new opportunities wait for us. To get these opportunities, we have to take our steps with strong determination and patience. And from here our new and powerful life begins.

7. Make this also one rule of life that whatever work you are starting, give it your 100% efforts. If you start doing it with your best, then a beautiful future is awaiting you. Thus, we have to determine that I have to get this goal.

8. Start celebrating the small happiness in life. Whether anyone appreciates you or not, you should pat your back and encourage yourself. Whenever you fail in your work,

take the responsibility and learning from this, move forward on a new path. There is no need of shame as no one gets complete success, until and unless he crosses the failures. This is life.

9. I have to remain positive always in my life. For this, I would have to adopt the method to learn managing myself in every problem, failure, or tension in every situation with positive thoughts. Then, any problems will be managed on their own. Because the solution of every problem is inside our mind 's thoughts.

10. Any type of challenge cannot put hurdles in my way. But if it does, that means I have accepted the defeat of that challenge. To live is life. It's true that there are losses and wins in life, but life never stops. We take our steps ahead by learning from these mistakes.

11. Any type of fear is my life's thinking. Fear has no actual existence. Always remember that fear always teaches us to move ahead as a challenge, to grow courage, create power. Whoever bows down to these fears, is devoid of life's power. If you think fear as your biggest enemy, then you will keep fighting with it and would be a winner. Because fear is born out of our thoughts and we have to destroy it.

12. There is a goldmine of happiness in our life. This is inside us so we have to wake up our happiness by ourselves only, and will try to make our life prosperous. For this, we will have to learn practice of Rajyog meditation for waking up our important and beneficial, creative and positive powers in the present time. If we learn this art in life then by doing this for few moments, we can learn to manage our life in simple ways. For this, we would have to take out some time for ourselves and it will be beneficial to manage our life's circumstances.

Chapter 6

Ikigai Food Culture

It is seen that the Japanese people are more fit and healthy than the rest of the world. They remain active in their work life long. Some people get surprised by their activities. How fit are the Japanese? You can guess by the fact that there are more aged people in Japan in the whole world. Let's know their secret of fitness.

They eat less in the night: It's seen that by taking a heavy diet in the night, your weight increases. This is because food doesn't have time to get digested. You must have heard the saying "Eat breakfast like a king, lunch like a prince, and dinner like a pauper." The biggest harm of eating a heavy dinner is that the danger of gaining weight increases. The Japanese don't do this. They eat very less in the night.

Drinking Green tea: Green tea is helpful in weight loss. It is antiviral and has antioxidants. The skin doesn't get wrinkled by consuming green tea. The Japanese take at least two cups of green tea. Let me tell you that Japanese tea leaves are thin, like needles, and are rich, dark coloured.

Breakfast is important: Let me tell you that in Japan breakfast is considered the most important time in the terms of health. In their breakfast green tea, steamed rice, tofu, miso soup, green onions, omelette and fish are included.

Eating Seafood: The Japanese really love to eat seafood.

The Japanese like seafood more than chicken, mutton or beef. They are very fond of eating fish because they reside near the sea coast. Japan consumes many thousand kilograms of seafood. Rich in protein, Omega 3 fatty acids, calcium, iron, vitamin C, fibre, beta carotene, fish saves them from many diseases.

Martial Arts: For the Japanese people, martial arts are a traditional game. In Japan both men and women compulsorily learn martial arts like judo, karate, and aikido. This keeps them fit.

Less Sweets: The Japanese eat food two-three times in a day but in low quantity. And, they eat sweets very seldom. They include 4-5 types of green vegetables in their food. Mostly they eat green and raw salads.

Exercise: Exercise is an important part of the Japanese daily life. In Japan all the people-- men or women, young and old, meditate. Doing meditation helps control tension, aids in living

longer. Besides these, cycling, reaming, long distance walk, and being active are included in their daily life chart.

On Sauna Hot Springs: The Japanese are very active. There is one more reason behind this-- that to keep their body beautiful and mind peaceful they take a special bath. It's known as Onsauna hot springs. In this, water is mixed with many nutrients, minerals and salts, which rejuvenate their body, mind and soul.

The Japanese use only traditional food in their breakfast. It includes specially Miso soup, steamed rice, vegetables and fish. Some people eat special Japanese omelette which is called "Tamagoyaki".

Okinawa and Ikigai: The residents of Okinawa in Japan are the longest living persons. Their average age is nearly 87 years. This is the place of people of age more than 110 years in population.

In Okinawa Japanese have different habits--Hari Hachi Boo. It is traditional for them to leave the dining table with 80% full stomach, without full content. It is believed that by practicing this, the Japanese have got good health results.

They eat many vegetables, both in quality and quantity. They also drink a lot of Sinpacha tea. It is a green tea and has jasmine and Shukuwasa Kinoo juice mixed in it. They eat very bitter food.

They do a lot of physical exercises, nothing too hectic. They have a busy life. They participate in clubs named Moss, practise meditation and keep their mind carefree and flexible.

They get such results only because of Ikigai, in which, there is a need for Japanese dedication and practice for keeping life lively with activities and motive. This is not about food or physical training, but a life style.

Studying Ikigai, you will find that food habits, exercises and other activities are greatly related to Ikigai. Without these, you will not be able to find your satisfactory life motive which you are searching.

Hara Hachi Boo: Many people don't know about the rules of 'Hara Hachi Boo' diet. Actually it is a Japanese eating routine to lowers body weight. Japanese are following this rule for many centuries. Perhaps, this is the reason that they seldom seen obese. If you also want to be fit and your body weight to be maintained, then start following this diet rule. Now, know everything about it.

What is Hara Hachi Boo?

Hara Hachi Boo is a Japanese sentence which means only 80% full stomach. This is Confucius's principle which teaches people to fill their stomach only 80%.

Okinawa People adopt Hara Hachi Boo

According to one study in the 21st century, Okinawa people's age is the longest in the world. They live up to 100 years. The reason of this is that the Okinawa people follow the Hara Hachi Boo diet. They take daily 1800 to 1900 calories. They fill their stomach only 80%.

Why Should One Follow Hara Hachi Boo?

According to the ancient Japanese diet culture, never fill the stomach 100%. Rather stop when it is 80% filled. According to the rule of Hara Hachi Boo, the digestive system takes a long time to digest food. It does cellular oxidation and people live longer. If the stomach is filled only 80%, the food is digested faster in an empty space. And, there are no health complexities.

Benefits of Hara Hachi Boo for Health

- It improves digestion.

- It helps in controlling body weight. It doesn't let the fat deposit on the waist and stomach.

- It saves people from obesity, gastrointestinal problems, acid reflux, and metabolic disorder.

- Hara Hachi Boo decreases free radicals in blood, thus it lowers the risk of cardiovascular diseases, cancer and age-related diseases.

How to follow Hara Hachi Boo

Eat slowly: A person eats more because of fast eating habits. Eat by chewing slowly. By this stomach gets full early and there would be no wish to eat more.

Focus on food: Turn off the TV, computer, mobile while eating. Focus only on the food while eating. If you eat slowly, you will eat less, and you will relish the food.

Eat in a small plate: Always use small plate and a narrow glass. This way you will eat less. For weight loss, Hara Hachi Boo rules are very effective. To get rid of obesity, fill your stomach only 80%. By this, your body and mind both will be healthy.

Will live upto 100 years: According to some studies of 21st century in Japan, the people's life of Okinawa is longest in the world. They live till 100 years. It happens, because they include Hara Hachi Boo regularly in their diet. In this way, they consume 1800 or 1900 calories daily. It has been believed as old Japanese food culture that one person should not fill his stomach more than 80%. This clearly means, there should be some empty space in the stomach. It makes digestion easy. So, here, people suffer less health problems.

There are many benefits for health by eating Hara Hachi Boo. It maintains health and well built body. Besides, it helps to prevent obesity, gastrointestinal disease, acid reflux and other diseases of the digestive system. And also, by eating this way regularly, the danger of heart diseases, cancer and other old age problems reduces.

Japanese Diet: People are most affected by their diets. There are calories in their food and very less sugar, so their weight doesn't increase. And, they are saved from diabetes, cholesterol, obesity, etc. Let's know what the Japanese people include in their diets to keep themselves healthy.

- **Seaweed and Seafood:** Vegetarian or non-vegetarian, the Japanese are very fond of sea food. It could be sea animals or sea vegetables, the Japanese love seafood. And vegetables of sea are ten times more powerful than the vegetables growing on the field. Besides, there are more nutrients in them than fish, chicken or meat.

Only Japan alone, eats 10% of the fish supplied to the world. The Japanese use around 1 lakh tonnes of seaweed each year. Seaweed has more quantities of iodine, and potassium. In only one cup of seaweed, there are 5 or 10 types of protein. And, there are vitamin B, vitamin C, Omega 3, iron, magnesium, calcium, zinc in good quantities.

It is also said the people using seafood are always remain young. Their skin becomes smooth. It makes hair also stays back till old age. And, the Japanese use very less milk and milk products. Because due to seafood they don't like milk, and there is no refined flour in their food either. They use mostly vegetables. That is why the Japanese people don't have stomach problems.

In Japan, rice is more eaten than bread. Japanese rice is also much better than ours, with white rice, brown and green rice varieties are also eaten.

Secret of Green Tea

Japan is such a country where much importance is given to tea. The country produces different types and different qualities of tea. There are teas which grow under the shade, another in steam, dried in sun, with buds, some barks, rice tea, sea algae tea, special tea cut on special days. How to grow tea and how they are produced, there are so many teas described to be had for different times.

Tea Culture in Japan

Tea culture developed around 1200 years ago in Japan. It was introduced by the Monk Eisai in the late 12th century. At that time, it was considered an expensive drink only for medicinal use.

Tea is the adventurous side of Japanese culture. For example, the Japanese tea festival turns tea preparation and consumption into an art. It is believed that the tea tree was brought from China around 805 years ago.

Shizuoka state is the biggest producer of tea in Japan. After that Kagoshima is the second state, Mei state is third and Miyazaki is the fourth state. In the ancient times tea was considered a luxury item and was used in temples and by important people only.

Now you can see tea stalls in every corner of Japan. There is tea everywhere—in vending machines, stores, and restaurants.

Types of Green Tea

The word tea is gained mainly from the Indian tree plant, which is known as green tea. Camille Sinosis or in Japanese, "Chanoki" or the main tea plant.

Chanoki (tea tree): This is a perennial tree which grows mainly in tropical or sub-tropical climate. Tree plants are grown from seeds or buds. One tree gives seeds in 4 to 12 years. One new tree is fit for cutting in approximately 3 years.

This is Indian tea or Camille Sinosis. This is the derivative of traditional green tea. Following this are different types of green tea and how to prepare them.

Ryokucha Green Tea: Ryokucha is the common name for green tea. There are different varieties in Japanese tea. In general, green tea is referred to only as tea or nihoncha (Japanese tea). We know it is much stronger than green tea.

Matka -- Grounded Green tea: Matka refers to powdered or grounded tea. This is used generally in tea festivals. It is used in sweets for colour and taste, and some food items also like Wagashio.

Genmaicha - Green Tea with Roasted Rice: Genmaicha is green tea with roasted rice. Historically it is the cheapest tea. Rice was for those people to fill the cup who could not afford pure tea. Today, it is admired for its unique taste and roasted aroma. Sometimes it has Matka in it.

Sencha Common Green Tea: Its name means ordinary tea and is important for every Japanese home. It has a very pleasant taste and aroma because all Japanese people steam their green tea for their natural flavour.

Kamaraicha Tea in Iron Pot: While most of the Japanese teas are made by steam, Kamaraicha is made in an iron pot at 300 Japanese C. So, its taste is less bitter and a little roasted.

Bancha - Cheap Tea: Bancha is green tea which is made with leaves harvested at the end of crop. It is a little smooth and a little bitter. It is a cheap tea generally served in Japanese restaurants. It is non-quantitative and of a low quality.

Benefits of Green Tea

The regular use of green tea by an adult not only prevent many diseases but also increases the immunity power against many diseases. Green tea works as an antioxidant along with anti-aging. The regular use of green tea is very beneficial to busy persons who are unable to exercise. Milk is not be mixed in it, because then the antioxidants become inactive. This tea is helpful in controlling cholesterol. Its use increases the fat burning in the body and metabolism. By using green tea, the brain tissues can be prevented from becoming dead. Green tea should be made by steaming.

Not only weight is controlled by green tea but the possibility of different diseases also decreases. By its use cancer can be prevented. In Japan, generally people drink tea with meals which helps in digestion and helps to prevent heart diseases.

According to studies, green tea is helpful for teeth also. It is preventive in viral, bacterial and throat infections. Green tea has polyphenols which prevent tooth cavities. Besides this, green tea is preventive in cancers of different kinds. The elements of green tea don't let cancer cells grow. Green tea prevents thrombosis also. It is anti-inflammatory, and has an effectiveness for pains also. Some antioxidants of green tea decrease the danger of arthritis. Green tea protects the liver in two ways. First, it protects the liver cells and secondly, it strengthens the immunity. In pregnancy, it gives the body iron, calcium, and magnesium. Regular tea should not be drunk in the night at sleeping time as it has caffeine. It increases hunger. On the other hand, you can drink green tea anytime even in night, as it has very low caffeine.

There is Theanine amino acid in green tea which decreases tensions. This controls the cortisol quantity which affects our mental tension directly, so we don't get tension.

❏

Chapter 7

Rhythmic Exercises

Japan is known as one of the world's biggest and most powerful countries. The Japanese life style is also very popular. Japan is very developed in technology. After the Second World War Japan's conditions were very bad. But in the next few years, it made so much progress that it became Asia's first developed country. The whole world is anxious to know the Japanese life style. The Japanese culture, dress, and people are popular all over the world. Japanese exercises are also popular.

It is well-known that the Japanese are very hard working. Japanese culture is identified with their working style. Generally, the Japanese people do work in overtime and holidays. Japanese people's thinking is that to do hard work is an example of good behaviour and like a training for life. The Japanese have really worked hard after the Second World War.

Sports of Japan

Sports are an important part in Japanese culture. In Japan, traditional games like Sumo wrestling and martial arts, and western games like baseball and football are very popular. Sumo wrestling has the status of a national sport. In the 19th century, after the Americans visited Japan, baseball entered the country.

In modern times, Japan has developed very systematic martial arts. In a collective form, it is still popular in Japan and other countries. In other sports, baseball, association football and other games are also played in Japan.

These games are specially practised in schools with traditional martial arts. The most popular games are baseball, football and table tennis. In 1991, the Japan professional football league was established. Japan had co-hosted the FIFA World Cup in 2002. Besides this, many semi-governmental organizations are working to encourage these sports. These are sponsored by private companies for games like volleyball, basketball, rugby, table tennis etc.

In the whole world Japan, was the first in technology, but this country is the leader in having a healthy population as well. This means that the Japanese are the healthiest people. They don't get obese and live a long life.

Though you will get machines for everything in Japan from walking to food, still people are much healthier than people of other countries. Because from their diet to their daily routine, the lifestyle of the Japanese is different from that of other countries. If we adopt their rules and diets, we would also be able to lead healthy life for long.

Japanese Exercises: You must have been trying different methods to get rid of obesity, but few methods are only workable and some are just a waste of time. By trying this Japanese technique, your belly fat will be lost within 2 days.

With this exercise not only will your body posture be corrected, your backache will also be taken care. Learn how to do these exercises.

Japanese Fukutsuji

Most of the people always fight with the weighing scales. It might be to get the thin waist of your dreams, but mostly

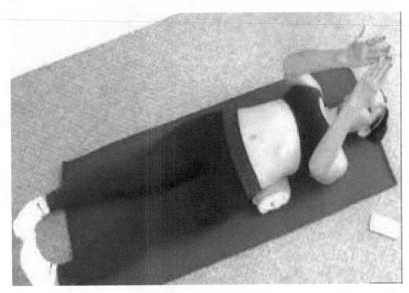

people take the support of crazy dieting, gym, and exercises. Others are very strict, and still others who search for costly and dangerous procedures. Even after using these alternatives, the expected results are not gained.

The Art of Knowing Fukutsuji

A Japanese doctor named Dr. Atoshiki Fukutsuji was the maker of this system. He is an expert in Reflexology, Shiatsu, and Acupuncture. This system is spreading not only in Japan but also all over the world. Many Youtubers and Bloggers also have tested the system, which is known as the exercise towel. The theory, according to the doctor, is that fat deposition in the stomach is due to wrong posture.

This exercise does the work of expanding the body, by which the bones return to its correct place. The more you repeat the exercise, the better results you will get. Along with reshaping the bones, the procedure makes the stomach muscles stronger. It finishes the fungal material stuck in the intestines. It reduces the extra weight on the very first day. Exercise distributes the body fat and improves the situation.

Step by Step Technical Fukutsuji

Wrap a towel on the cylindrical rollers. Safely tie with ribbon or a string etc.

- Lie down on the towel at some flat and solid place.
- Fit the rolling pin in the towel on your navel.
- Raise your legs at the level of your shoulders and touch the toes.
- Raise your arms above your head, lower your palms and touch the fingers.
- Stay in this position for approx. 5 minutes. Complete the exercises slowly in a calm manner.

Reduce the Tummy Fat with Japanese Techniques

Whenever you talk about tummy fat, it is very difficult to reduce it. You would need to try for more. You will have to work hard on your tummy. Recently one Japanese technique has come out by which you can reduce tummy fat. With this method, in Japan, one person has lost 13kg weight and 4/7 inches of tummy. Before this, it was possible only with hard work and exercise.

1. Stand straight, take out one leg forward, and put the other leg back.
2. Tight your butts and put your body weight on your back leg.
3. Raise your arms above your head. Breathe, inhaling slowly for 3 seconds.
4. Exhale for 7 seconds, put tension on your muscles.

Yoga

If you feel that yoga means twisting your body in different ways, now is the time for you to rethink. Yoga is not limited to asanas, but it is much more than this. It could be said in simple way that it takes care of the mind, body and breathing.

The word Yoga is made of 'Yuj'. Which means to join or assemble. Yoga is an important part of Indian Gyanpeetha for more than 5000 years. In yoga, we learn to balance different body parts through asanas, pranayam, and meditation.

Motive of Yoga

Yoga is an art of living. It is a meditation science. It has an important place in human life. Knowledge has been given importance in its meditation and theories. By yoga, spiritual and physical development is possible. How to become tension free at every step and how to get peace and harmony? To disclose this secret is the main motive of yoga.

The main motive of yoga is learning to build such persons whose emotional level would be enlightened with divine values, belief and planning. So that their thoughts should be like God's devotees and yogis. Because in such persons, the capabilities and aura is of a high grade. Definitely in comparison to ordinary persons they are best capable, and they plan that the energy flows to develop their subconscious. We can be successful in taking an active mind to a calm and serene state with the help of fasting, beliefs, and meditation like practices.

If we look into different subjects of yoga, we find that the object of Hathyoga meditation is to control the obstruction of the mind caused by the physical body. We have to build a healthy body controlling nerves. If we come to Ashtanga yoga, we find the real motive of the rule of yoga is to remove the causes of tension - greed, illusion, lust, attachments etc.

The main motive of yoga, asanas and pranayama is to remove the physical body's distractions. The main motive is to distract the mind from the worldly pleasures to inner wisdom. The motive of belief is to distract the mind from all the pleasure and meditate in special state. When it is stable it is called meditation and the extreme of meditation is the samadhi to experience oneness with the universe. In the highest stage of samadhi one can visualize God's true form, which is the ultimate goal of humans according to ancient wise men.

Aims of Yoga

- to develop mental power.
- to develop creativity.
- to get rid of tensions.
- to improve anti nature life style.
- to develop broad viewpoint.
- to get mental peace.
- to develop best physical capacities.
- to get rid of physical diseases.
- to get rid of alcohol and other toxicity.
- to achieve divine transformation of human.

Types of Yoga

The methods adopted by the persons to reach the ultimate stage of samadhi, moksha, are described in yoga books from time to time. These are known as different types of yoga.

1. **Hathayoga:** In the ancient times, there was a well-known saint Gherand, who was an expert in Hathayoga. He created "Gherand Samhita" for the practical teaching of this form to his disciple Chandakpali. It is still

available. This is an authentic and recognized book. In this book, the seven parts of Hathayoga (shatkarma asana, mudra, pratyaahar, pranayama, dhyan, samadhi) are described in depth.

Speciality in Hathayoga: This also includes physical activities. Gourakshnathji has put a thrust on many mudras for the correct "Shatchakra Bhedan" of the body. For example- Kaki mudra (sucking oxygen by twisting tongue like a crow's beak, Khechari mudra (sucking air by pulling back tongue to the end in the throat, then doing 84 asanas—like Moolbandh, Usrian bandh, Jalandhar bandh, etc.

2. **Laya Yoga:** Yoga teachers have considered rythm also a method of reaching to God. It means "tune your heart with your soul, diffuse it." *Anand ta: pashyani vidvansasten layen pashyanti*" The wise ones looking for Anand Swaroop (the soul) tuned themselves into it, after this they don't see anything in the universe separately. So, by this, man reaches to the soul by searching for truth with knowledge. Now he finds out that not only his soul, but all the universe is diffused in it. That soul is the super soul of God. Both are one. They are no different from each other. This is laya yoga.

3. **Rajyoga:** *"Rajatvat sarvyoganam rajyog iti smrat:"* In the scriptures, it is said that the best among all the yoga methods and being the king of all yoga activities, it is called Rajyoga. Dhyan of Rajyog is said to be Brahma Dhyan, Samadhi is Nirvikalp samadhi, and the expert of Rajyoga is called the perfect mahatma, free of life. The most authentic scripture about Rajyoga is the Yogadarshan, written by Maharishi Patanjali. It is said that by removing the mind's fluttering, perceptual side of

Yoga and Siddha yoga, and concentrating and stabilizing the mind in the practice of the diffusion of soul to God, you can practise Rajyoga. This was told by Lord Brahma to the Rishis through the Vedas.

Some yoga teachers have considered Rajyoga completed with sixteen arts, means considered to have sixteen parts. Seven parts have knowledge, two types of concepts- Natural concepts and Brahma concepts, three types of meditation- Virat Dhyan, Eish Dhyan, Brahma Dhyan, four types of samadhi - two with good thoughts and two with no thoughts (Vitarka anugat, Vichar anugat, Anand anugat, Asmita anugat). The person doing meditation in this sequence gets free of life after reached his form.

5. **Bhakti Yoga:** Nishkaam karma means only do your work without desiring the results. Following the Bhakti Marg, the person feels God's presence. It is said in the Gita *"Patram pushpam falam toshanyo me bhaktya prachyati"* which means if any devotee offers me even leaves, flowers, and water with love, I accept those happily.

5. **Gyan Yoga:** In the world there is nothing as sacred as knowledge. In the Gita it is said *"Nahi gyanen sadrashampavitrmih vidyate."* There are two types of knowledge --rational knowledge and spiritual knowledge. Rational knowledge is known as science, this is done for truth represented in things. It has the knowledge of the learned and learner. Spiritual knowledge is known as knowledge. In this, there is no difference between the learned and learner. Such a person can visualize God in every form.

6. **Karma Yog:** *"Yagyartha karmanoanyatra lokoyam karmbandhana:"* ---Gita - *"Taksharth karm kountaya*

muktasang:" samachar: yog and sidhdhayog's concept says this world is tied with the chains of actions. "So. Oh Arjuna! You do your action. Swaymyagya, the horns of karma. Grains are produced in farms by action. Arjun, you do your action without attachment. Because a Yogi does the action for the purity of the soul. Everyone has to do the action compelled by nature. There is no freedom without getting the results of own's reaction."

7. **Japa Yoga:** Japa is the name of one divine power or mantra. According to Swami Shivananda, "Japa is an important part of yoga." In this Kalyuga, only Japa can give eternal peace, superior pleasure, and immortality. One should be a Japa expert and should do Japa with morality, purity, love and adoration. There is no bigger yoga than Japa yoga. It can give you everything-- whatever you want—Sat Sidhdhi, Bhakti, Mukti.

8. **Ashtanga Yoga:** Maharishi Patanjali had started Patanjali Yoga Darshan with the word "Athyog anushasnam." So, it is clear how much importance he has given to discipline in life's principles. Patanjali Yoga is done in eight sequences. So, it is called Ashtanga yoga. There are eight parts of the Ashtanga yoga :

   1. Yama

   2. Niyam

   3. Asanas

   4. Pranayama

   5. Pratyahar

   6. Dharana

   7. Dhyan

   8. Samadhi

Before practising the above eight parts, a person has to do Shatkarma compulsorily. Shatkarma are told as follows :

1. Neti

2. Nouli

3. Dhouti

4. Basti

5. Kapaal

6. Bhaati

7. Traatak

Benefits of Yoga

Along with practising yoga one should do meditation, deep breathing, and control the breathing. According to the Patanjali Yoga Sutra, Yoga keeps mind peaceful. In other words, yoga slows down disappointments, sorrow, anger, and fear, which can cause tension. Tension is the root of all the health problems, in which migraine, sleeplessness, heart diseases are included. If you learn to keep your mind peaceful, you will be healthy for a long time.

Internal Health Benefits of Yoga

Blood Circulation: When blood circulation in body is improved, then all the organs work better. The body temperature also remains controlled. As blood circulation gets uncontrollable, the body falls victim to different diseases. Like heart diseases, a bad liver, the brain not functioning properly, etc. are all situations of ill-health. In this situation, the blood circulates properly only by doing yoga. By this, all the organs of body get oxygen and nutrients.

Balanced Blood Pressure: Many people are suffering of blood pressure problems due to a wrong lifestyle. If you also have some blood pressure problems, start from today—begin yoga under the supervision of yoga teacher. Yoga is important also because doing pranayama will provide the body with enough energy and the nervous system will work better. The heartbeat also gets normal.

Better Respiratory System: Any abnormality in respiratory system is enough to make us unwell. In this situation, yoga tells us the how important breathing is for life, because every yogasana is based on breathing. When you do yoga, then the lungs work with full capacity, making breathing easy.

Relief from Indigestion: In the other benefits of yoga relief from gas due to indigestion is also included. Anybody can have gas problems, including children, old age people. This problem arises because of the digestive system not working properly. To correct this problem, yoga is the best cure. Yoga makes the digestive system better and we can get rid of the problems like indigestion, gas, acidity, etc.

Power to bear the pain: In the body, there could be pains anywhere, anytime. Especially the joint pains are unbearable. When you begin doing yoga, in the beginning, the physical capacity increases to bear the pains. After regular practice the pains reduce.

Immunity Power: To fight with diseases, your immunity capabilities should be better. The body falls victim of several diseases if the immunity is weak. Whether you are healthy or not, in both conditions, doing yoga would be a beneficial bargain. Your immunity power will get stronger.

New Energy: To live life positively and working energy in the body is very important. In this yoga helps you. Tiredness gets over by doing yoga and body fills up with new energy.

Better Metabolism: For our body metabolic reactions are important. Our body gets energy from food by this reaction only, so we are able to do our daily work normally. When the digestive system, liver, and kidney are working properly, metabolism works better. In this context, yoga is beneficial because through yoga indigestion can be cured and the metabolism made better.

Sleep: After working the whole day, it is important to have good sleep in the night. It helps the body to get ready for the next day's work. Not taking sufficient sleep would result in restlessness, headache, eyes burning, and tension. There won't be any glow on the face. On the other hand, when you do yoga, your mind becomes peaceful, gets rid of tension, and you get a good sleep in the night.

Balanced Cholesterol: Like we had told before, blood circulation gets better by doing yoga. Because of it, there is also a better blood flow in the body. So, there wouldn't be the problem of blood clots and extra fats. This is the reason we can control cholesterol. Yoga increases good cholesterol (HDL) and decreases bad cholesterol (LDL). Along with balance diet, exercise like yoga is also necessary.

Control of Sodium: Often, we eat spicy or junk food from outside. In these foods, the sodium level is always very high. With an increased sodium in the body, heart diseases or liver diseases can attack us. To avoid this, firstly you should stop eating this type of food. Simultaneously, do yoga regularly. Yoga is capable of controlling sodium levels.

Reduced Triglycerides: Triglycerides are one type of fat in our blood, which could be cause of heart disease or stroke. To reduce it, regular yoga is very necessary. By doing yoga heartbeats usually increased, so, triglycerides like situation can be prevented.

Prevention of Heart Diseases: The heart is a delicate part of our body. The diet, an unbalanced lifestyle and tensions directly affect our heart. There would be heart diseases in the future. Yoga is the best preventive. Regular yoga and a healthy diet keep the heart stronger. You will understand the value of yoga, when you practise for your heart.

Increased in RBC: There is huge contribution of RBCs in our body. They take oxygen from our lungs and supply it to every part of body. Deficiency of RBCs may lead to Anaemia. By doing yoga, its quantity increases.

Asthma: In asthma, the respiratory tract gets shrunk, so it is difficult to breathe. We suffocate in little dusty areas. If you do yoga in this condition, then your lungs get under pressure and they work better with high efficiency.

Arthritis: In arthritis, the joints swell and get painful. In this condition, it is very difficult to do daily chores. In this situation, yoga could be very beneficial for you. Doing yoga under the supervision of a yoga teacher can help in joint pains and thus the swelling gradually reduced and they start working.

Cancer: It is difficult to say that if cancer gets fully cured from yoga or not. But yes, it can be surely said that with yoga it's helpful to come out of cancer. By doing yoga, toxic bacteria in the cancer patient's body start reducing and blood circulation gets better. There is less tension and tiredness. Along with nausea and vomiting, that is caused by chemotherapy, could be managed.

Migraine: If a migraine patient does yoga, he could get relieved of pain in the head. Yoga reduces the muscles tensions, and brain gets proper oxygen supply, so the patient get relieved of headache.

Bronchitis: The air passage of the mouth, nose and lungs is called the respiratory tract. When it gets swollen, breathing becomes difficult. In medical language, it is known as bronchitis. Yoga helps you to remove this swelling. Through yoga, oxygen is supplied fully to the lungs, and simultaneously the lungs get recharged with energy.

Constipation: This is the disease which is the root cause of many diseases. Constipation happens due to problems in the digestive system. To cure it, yoga is better than medicine. With yoga, constipation can be rooted out. First of all, yoga will cure the digestive system, so constipation will cure itself and you will feel fresh.

Infertility and Menopause: If someone wants to better her fertility, there are many asanas described in yoga. By doing yoga, any sperm-related problem, any sex problem, fallopian tube issues and PCOD can be cured. Other than this, pre or post menopause, any negative signs can also be cured through yoga.

Sinus and other Allergies: Because of Sinus, the muscles around the nose get swollen. This causes trouble in breathing. To solve this problem also, yoga is the better solution. In Sinus, doing breathing related yoga exercises, like Pranayama, remove the obstacles in the nose and throat's tubes and breathing becomes easier. Besides these, other allergies can also be cured with yoga.

Low Back Pain: In today' time, our most of the work is done while sitting. Because of this, everyone has a low back pain at some stage. If you do yoga under the guidance of an able yoga teacher, then the backbone becomes flexible, with this, any kind of back pain can be removed.

External Benefits of Yoga

Less effect of aging: Some people's face shows the early aging signs. If you do yoga, then aging before time can be controlled. Through yoga, toxic agents and bacteria are cleaned out of the body and free radicals are also cleared up. Because of tension also, early aging signs reflects. But yoga prevents from all these situations.

Increased Physical Power: Sitting and walking in the wrong posture causes wrong body structure. Because of this, there can be pain in different body parts, and due to which muscles and bones get weaker. To be preventive of these diseases, the right step is to practise yoga. With regular practise of yoga bones and muscles get stronger. The body gets in better shape and physical power increases.

Balanced Body Weight: These days most of the people are victim of obesity. The cause of this is a wrong diet and wrong lifestyle. First of all, our stomach suffers. A bad digestive system is the root cause of all diseases. The best and easy method to deal with this is yoga. If you do regular yoga, then problems like constipation and acidity are cured and the digestive system gets better. Because of this even the weight gets decreased.

A Well-Built Body: Yogasana makes the body balanced from head to toe, and makes you mentally and spiritually stronger. The proper functioning of the organs makes your body fit and fine.

Increase of Core Power: The Core is the main group of important muscles of the body. For the body's correct functioning, it is important that core should be developed to be stronger. The entire body weight leans on the core. This protects you from getting hurt. Doing yoga makes the core get stronger, healthier and with more flexibility.

Improvement in Muscles: Muscles activities also get improved by yoga. Muscles gets stronger and flexible.

Develops of Tolerance: As written very often in the book, yoga makes a person stronger, not only physically but mentally also. It is required on daily basis. Specially sports players need to be mentally stronger to win. The more they stay tolerant, their performance gets better. Simultaneously, everyone is able to take right decisions even in adverse conditions if they have a strong mental makeup.

Chapter 8

Worry and Tension

Worry is a physical and psychological condition, made up of special components which include cognitive, physical, and psychological behaviour. These components join to make an unpleasant psyche, which is generally related to anxiety, fear, apprehension, and distress. Worry is generally a mood which can be borne out of unknown sources. If it could be seen that it is different from fear, which is borne out of known danger. Apart from this, fear is related especially to the behaviour of avoiding and running away, whereas worry is the results of uncontrollable and unavoidable dangers.

Another view is that "worry is a mood facing the future in which a person is willing or getting ready for future negative incidents." This suggests that there are differences between future versus present danger, which divides fear and worry. Worry is known as a normal reaction of tension. This can help a person to deal with any difficult situations, at work or school encouraged by others to strongly face these problems. Too much worrying can become the cause of anxiety disorders for a person.

In today's rushing world, there are so many worries in life. But to get rid of these worries, it is not correct to take help of medicines. Prem Kumar Sharma mentions some methods to get rid of worries.

You may not have realized, but in worrisome conditions, your heartbeats get faster. Breaths begin to go up and down. So, whenever there is situation of worry and problems, you must control your breathing. In this way, you inhale ten deep long breaths and exhale. By doing this, your heartbeat would become normal and you will be tension free.

If you really want to manage your worries, then try to know the cause of the worry. Note it down on paper. Then think, what could be the solution of this problem? If possible, begin working on it immediately.

Sometimes phobia or fear also becomes the cause of worry, so try to control the fear. In this time start thinking about those things which give you peace. For example, listening to music, praying, exercise, reading, or simply sitting in a relaxed manner, etc. It is said that 'victory is beyond fear'. And this is correct too.

Self-confidence is the best quality for anyone to have. If your self confidence is high, then you can stay cool in any circumstances.

Often, we try to be perfect and due to this we surround ourselves with worries. So, it is considered best that one should try to give his best. Simultaneously, will subside if you are working with a positive attitude.

If you are unable to fight alone with your problems, then share your problems with someone. For this, you could take help from an anxiety support group. If the person is really your well-wisher, then you can feel peaceful by telling him about your problems unhesitatingly.

If we are surrounded with worries, then we don't take care of ourselves in this period, causing our lifestyle to be disrupted. And problems grow more rather than ending. So, in this time it would be best to take care of yourselves. A correct diet, having good sleep, will keep you safe from other problems. The whole idea is that you should not be careless in anxiety, rather stay careful.

Thinking about the future is an invitation to problems. So, live in the present, keep trying to make it better, that's why many support groups have their slogan as "one day at a time." Each new day teaches us so many new things, and teaches us to fight with our problems.

It's quite natural that when a person is surrounded with problems and worries, his health is directly affected. If you save yourself from this situation, then you will be free from future problems. So, to be tension free, you should keep yourself active and busy. This means don't let your worries affect your daily routine. This will keep your mind active and soon you will get solution of your problems.

Sometimes your routine itself becomes the cause of your worries. So, little changes in it would be beneficial for you, barring its effect on your important work.

And if you have adopted all the methods and still, they are not benefiting you, and you are forced to be worrisome, then you could take medical help. But instead of taking medicines some therapy or meditation will also be beneficial. One motto for you should be "Don't Give Up". Face the problem and fight them, then only your life will be peaceful.

Do Constructive Work

Senior clinical psychologist of Fortis Escorts Institute and Research Centre, Dr. Bhavna Barmi says that if one could make their life constructive, then they can get rid of worries to a large

extent. Give importance to positive aspects in your lifestyle and forget negativity totally. If life is positive, anxiety would be less. You can cut down your worries by doing exercise.

Simultaneously, it would be right to have daily, controlled diet on time. Try to have a balanced diet, eating three times in a day and including two snacks. Food plays very important role in making our body fit and healthy. So, we have to ensure that our food should be nutritious and devoid of junk food. As junk food only spoils our digestive system and thus makes us obese. That's why exercise on daily basis is must.

Along with this, drinking enough water also gets rid of worries. If you start your day with one glass of water, it would be best.

You can make your hobby also an alternative to remove your worries. If you enjoy book reading, playing, listening to music, or other hobbies, then you will get rid of worries in any worrying times. Or you can talk to your family face-to-face, to discuss whatever is on your mind to make yourself tension free. Your attention would be on new projects, giving you relaxation.

Deep breathing is also a simple but effective technique to remove the worries. Whenever you are under stress or mental tension, take a deep long breath. First inhale a deep long breath, hold it, and exhale. Repeat this with ease.

Tension Free with Meditation

Have you found yourself in the middle of an unknown fear and danger of a bad incident? Experiment this once. Tight your fists as tight as you can, now open your fist. What was easy? Tighten the fist or opening? Simple, to open is much easier and relaxing. But mostly people tighten their fears and troubles.

We all want to leave our worries. But, how much do we try to put ourselves in a situation that there is no use of worries, we can't stop ourselves away from them. We don't know what to do, so in this article we have talked about some less popular but effective methods to get rid of worries.

Meditation to reduce Worry and Tensions

Have you ever thought about meditation to get rid of worries? They could be due to many causes like work pressures, sickness, insufficient food, bad sleeping habits, emotional pressure, hyper sensitivity towards noise, different fears, etc. Sometimes, there is a pressure to achieve everything soon. Whatever be the reason, meditation is one of the best methods to get rid of worries.

When you meditate, you give rest your distressed heart. Tension activates your internal tension hormones, which keeps

you worried. Regular meditation reduces this internal hormone, so you feel better. What do you lose after meditation? —only tensions. But you have to be sure to do it regularly. With daily meditation, you will have the feelings of growing feeling of trust and freedom from within. So, do try it once. The remedy you are searching to get free of tension can be found in meditation.

"Sajag Dhyan" –For Keeping Tension Free

By practising "Sajag Dhyan" you remain active towards your feelings, emotions and thoughts without attaching any goodness or badness, so that you could handle it. This is the amazing way to reduce the tensions. This determines that you are the controller of emotions and not vice versa.

Meditation and Yoga

1. Tips for Good Sleep: If you have a problem in sleeping at nights, there is a kind of meditation for good sleep, which will take you to sleep without any medication.

2. Enthusiasm is a method in itself to crossover worries : Do you remember going to your best friend's birthday party in childhood? What fun it was to be among the happy people, full of enthusiasm and excitement? You used to like it so much that you never wanted to come back from there. Those were the tension free moments. After all, you couldn't do both together to worry and to celebrate with enthusiasm.

It's so easy to understand that when we get together to do something, we get enthusiastic. We get energy within us which removes all the worries which comes due to lack of energy. This is the simple and natural method to remove the worries.

Gurudev Shri Shri says, "Life is love. Life is pleasure. Life is excitement." With regular practice of meditation your mind becomes peaceful. And you simply feel that life is a festival, which is filled with love, pleasure, and excitement.

Your cause of worry could be imbalanced hormones too. So, do consult some doctor or seek ayurvedic or homeopathic solutions if you feel allopathic medicines would have bad effects.

3. Advice for food: It is very important to pay attention to your food intake. Take mostly fresh, healthy vegetarian food. Drink lots of water. Eat only when you feel hungry. Do at least 20 minutes yoga daily to keep your body and mind in fit shape, along with daily meditation. Doing meditation on an empty stomach is beneficial.

4. Expand your worries: Are you entangled in relationships? Or are tensed for not having an increased income? Are your competitors leaving you behind? Gurudev Shri Shri says, "We should worry about the whole world, not only for ourselves." To worry is human. So, why not worry for the welfare of more people? In reality, there wouldn't be any welfare with worrying, but yes, doing something could make some changes. Doing some work takes you beyond worrying. When you look at the vast exposure, then our worries seem tiny. This thought is a boon in itself. And this is the simple method to get free of tension.

Would you like to know how selfless service gets you tension free? There are less fortunate people who can't enjoy life like you. So, the small step taken by you could bring big changes in their life. To know that you are the reason for someone's happiness, fills you with extreme pleasures. This enthusiasm helps you to keep away from negativity. To teach some needy child, or get the medicine for poor are some small works done by you which can bring big changes in those people's life.

Do meditation after the service or you would feel tired. Meditation done after service gives deep experiences.

Tips for Instant Relief from Fear and Worry

Do meditation to get instant relief from fear and worry. You can do it anywhere. With regular practice of yoga, you will get early relief from fear and worry. Have you done any meditation today? If not, then do it now. Learn more about Sahaj yoga and practise it regularly.

Tension is only a mental condition: Actually, tension is nothing but a mental condition which is born out of incidents imagined by our mind. The unfair pressure on the mind makes the situations for tension, worry, and nervousness. If we haven't prepared to face some special situations, then also we feel tensed. Past experiences of some special problems also cause tensions.

If we had tensions earlier because of certain problems, then facing the same problems we again get tensed. Gradually, it becomes our habit to remain tensed and worrying. So, there are different causes in life to get tensed, and these causes keep changing as per time and person. Let's try to find out that if we are victim of tension then what could we do to keep it away. As we know tension is a mental condition. So, how do we make our mind tension free? There is urgent need to pay attention to this subject.

Find out the Causes of Tension

Once when you get successful to find out the causes of your tension, then you can handle it in a better way. The cause of tension could be some special person or incident. To find out the solution of your tension you would have to adopt innovative methods. It's quite possible that you will be tension free with these small steps.

Learn to ignore: Our emotional attachment with some things gets too much and we get tensed. You should remember that it is not necessary that you are always right. Everyone has a right to keep his opinions and no need to argue about it with anyone.

Just understand that the person is viewing the special situations differently due to his biased thoughts than your opinions. Just thinking this, you can come out of tensed situations easily. There could be different ways to achieve some special goal, so think about the other ways also along with yours. And try to find out the best solution.

Only present time matters: Nothing lasts forever. Whoever is here, could be somewhere else tomorrow. So, try to avoid tensions. Search for the opportunities in the problems instead getting tensed. The developed art of converting adverse situations into favourable ones will be beneficial for you in the future.

Remember your tension will affect you but the situations causing your tensions will change itself with time. A short time situation could cause unnecessary tension which would have a long term physical, mental, and emotional effect on you.

Be Optimistic: Often, we get tensed imagining the worst. Though it is not necessary that bad situations getting worse, it is a possibility that nothing worse would happen in future. It is said that every life has self-predictions, so think positively. If you think good and good things will come.

Look at the world around you alongwith looking at yourself: If you always focus your attention towards your life and its issues, definitely you will be tensed. So, come out of your web of problems and look around the world. Observe others and their life aspects. If you keep crying over your problems, they would become giant-size.

So, it's important that you divert your mind from your problems and look for other's problems and try to solve them. The attempt to solve others' problems will make you more tolerant with time. And, you will be able to dedicate your life to make others happy. At last, whatever work you do, relay your thoughts, you will get the results accordingly.

Don't get angry: Anger is your biggest enemy. It could burst easily anytime, and if it gets violent, it's hard to pacify. We should remember that after the anger subsides, there is nothing left than repentance. It is well said that there is no use crying over spilt milk. Could spilled milk get back? Mostly, anger is the cause of any sudden health disruption. We can have long time chronic diseases also due to anger.

Getting angry with yourself or with others will give negative results only. Because of anger, there come tensions in relationships, sometimes causing breakups. Keep your mind cool to stay away of anger, and find the problem's solution. No situations are without solutions. Analyse life's situations and differences of opinions. Accept your life's speciality and situations.

Start writing a 'tension description': Tension descriptions will help you to identify and solve the problems. Whenever you feel tensed, note down the description of how you are feeling. You will get the idea of tension's pattern and other general ideas with daily writing. Describe these as follows:

- Cause of the tension (if not correctly identified, then guess)?
- How do you feel physically and mentally?
- How do you react?
- Identifying doing what makes you feel better?
- Think about how did you solve the problems recently.

You can identify the issues from your description. Are you using the right methods or you are using unhealthy, uncreative ways? Unfortunately, people adopt such methods to deal with tensions that their problems grow more.

Accept the things beyond your control: Some sources of tensions are mandatory. You can't run away from them and can't change them. For example, in case of a death in the family, any chronic disease, or depression. The best way to come out of the tension of these situations, is to accept as it is. Obviously, it would be difficult but it would be easier and beneficial to accept rather than avoiding the situation for longer period.

Don't try to control the things beyond your reach. There are some things which are beyond control in life- especially other people's behaviour. Rather than being tensed over these, it would be better if you concentrate on such things which you could control such as the opportunity which you choose to solve the problems.

Always look ahead. It is said "What doesn't kill you, makes you stronger." Facing the bigger challenges, you should look at them as an opportunity at a personal level. If your wrong selection makes you a victim of tension, then think over and learn from your mistakes.

Share your feelings. Talk to reliable persons. Or consult some therapist. If you share your feelings with others, then you will feel better about the situation, even if you can't change it.

Learn to forgive: Accept the fact that we are living in an incomplete world, where people make mistakes repeatedly. Take the anger and unpleasantness out of yourselves. By forgiving others you become free of negativity and move ahead. If you take time out for enjoyment and relaxation regularly, then you could deal with your causes of tensions very well.

CPSIA information can be obtained
at www.ICGtesting.com
Printed in the USA
LVHW041456150422
716311LV00004B/280